The 369 Manifestation Guide and Journal

Bring Your Dreams to Life with the Power of Numbers

© Copyright 2025 - All rights reserved.

The content contained within this book may not be reproduced, duplicated, or transmitted without direct written permission from the author or the publisher.

Under no circumstances will any blame or legal responsibility be held against the publisher or author for any damages, reparation, or monetary loss due to the information contained within this book, either directly or indirectly.

Legal Notice:

This book is copyright-protected. It is only for personal use. You cannot amend, distribute, sell, use, quote, or paraphrase any part of the content within this book without the consent of the author or publisher.

Disclaimer Notice:

Please note that the information contained within this document is for educational and entertainment purposes only. All effort has been executed to present accurate, up-to-date, reliable, and complete information. No warranties of any kind are declared or implied. Readers acknowledge that the author is not engaging in the rendering of legal, financial, medical, or professional advice. The content within this book has been derived from various sources. Please consult a licensed professional before attempting any techniques outlined in this book.

By reading this document, the reader agrees that under no circumstances is the author responsible for any losses, direct or indirect, that are incurred as a result of the use of the information contained within this document, including, but not limited to, errors, omissions, or inaccuracies.

Your Free Gift
(only available for a limited time)

Thanks for getting this book! If you want to learn more about various spirituality topics, then join Mari Silva's community and get a free guided meditation MP3 for awakening your third eye. This guided meditation mp3 is designed to open and strengthen ones third eye so you can experience a higher state of consciousness. Simply visit the link below the image to get started.

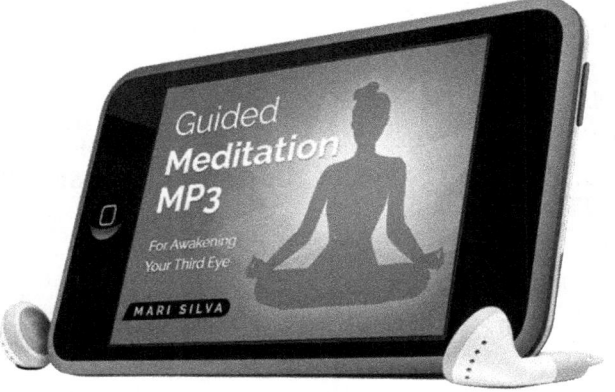

https://spiritualityspot.com/meditation

Or, Scan the QR code!

Table of Contents

PART 1: 369 MANIFESTATION 1
   INTRODUCTION 3
   CHAPTER 1: THE ORIGIN OF 369: NIKOLA TESLA'S SECRET CODE TO THE UNIVERSE 5
   CHAPTER 2: START WITH SETTING INTENTIONS 11
   CHAPTER 3: MANIFESTING LOVE WITH 369 21
   CHAPTER 4: USING 369 FOR MONEY, ABUNDANCE, AND SUCCESS 32
   CHAPTER 5: 369 FOR EMOTIONAL AND PHYSICAL WELL-BEING 42
   BONUS: 369 MANIFESTATION ROUTINES 52
   CONCLUSION 61
PART 2: 369 MANIFESTATION JOURNAL 63
   INTRODUCTION 65
   START YOUR 369 PRACTICE 67
   SECTION 1: BEGIN 68
   ATTRACT ABUNDANCE DAILY 75
   SECTION 2: ABUNDANCE 76
   INVITE LOVE INTO YOUR LIFE 85
   SECTION 3: LOVE 86
   FUEL FINANCIAL SUCCESS 97
   SECTION 4: WEALTH 98
   MANIFEST INNER PEACE 109

SECTION 5: EMOTIONAL WELL-BEING 110
CONCLUSION 118
HERE'S ANOTHER BOOK BY MARI SILVA THAT YOU MIGHT
LIKE 120
YOUR FREE GIFT (ONLY AVAILABLE FOR A LIMITED TIME) 121
REFERENCES 122
IMAGE SOURCES 132

Part 1: 369 Manifestation

Master the Secret Code to Manifest Love, Money, Abundance, Healing, and Positive Transformation

Introduction

Manifestation is not a magic lamp you can rub to enable a genie to come out and grant you three wishes. It is a philosophical concept that highlights the power of positivity and explains how it can bring you positive experiences. It aligns your energy and thoughts with the universe to bring your desires to fruition. You can achieve anything when you change your perspective and believe in yourself. While there are different manifestation methods, Nikola Tesla's 369 code stands out and has proven effective.

The book begins by exploring Nikola Tesla's 369 code and explains why he believed that these numbers held the key to understanding reality. You will also discover their significance and how Tesla's theory aligns with different universal laws.

Intentions are powerful and can be considered a crucial part of manifestation. You'll learn their role in the 369 method and how they can strengthen self-belief and bring positivity. If you have not discovered your goals yet, you'll find techniques to help you uncover your passion. You will also understand how to use intentions with the 369 Method.

Some people don't know how to use intentions, which is why they often fail to work. The book explains the common mistakes people make when setting intentions and how to avoid them.

The 369 Method can help you attract many positive things in your life. You'll discover how to use this technique to manifest love. Different strategies, like visualization, can prepare your mindset and manifest positive emotions. You will also understand the impact of affirmation and emotional connection on strengthening the power of manifestation.

Limiting beliefs and self-doubt can prevent you from achieving your goals. The book teaches you how to recognize and reframe negative thoughts and beliefs to attract success. You'll also learn the importance of openness and gratitude to help you align your mindset with the energy of abundance.

The last part of the book focuses on emotional and physical well-being. It explores how this method can strengthen mental health, heal the body, and bring peace. Practical exercises at the end of each chapter help you apply what you have learned.

This book stands out because it focuses on the 369 Method without all the fluff. All the information and strategies are explained in simple terms, making it ideal for beginners. It also includes a bonus section on routines to help you incorporate the 369 Method into every aspect of your life.

Begin your journey now and discover how the power of manifestation can change your life.

Chapter 1: The Origin of 369: Nikola Tesla's Secret Code to the Universe

What is the first thing that comes to mind when you hear "Nikola Tesla"? You probably think of his scientific contributions, such as the Tesla coil, a high-frequency alternating current that impacted wireless technology and changed the world. Tesla was an engineer and an inventor, a man of science that one can only associate with pragmatic and theoretical thinking.

However, Tesla's contributions also extended to manifestation and the laws of attraction. He used his knowledge of physics and numerology to create the mystical 369 code, which became a powerful manifestation method.

Nikola Tesla.[1]

This chapter introduces the 369 Method, its numerological significance, and its connection to universal laws. It explores how Tesla's work connects scientific and spiritual concepts, proving his theory's credibility. You will also discover the impact of his ideas on modern manifestation techniques.

What Is Manifestation?

Manifestation involves transforming your thoughts, ideas, goals, desires, and dreams into reality using techniques such as intentions and visualization. It is based on the belief that you attract what you think. Understandably, some people may be skeptical about manifestation and use scientific theories to argue the validity of spiritual concepts. However, manifestation is different since many of its techniques are taken directly from psychology or science, such as the 369 Method. Manifestation focuses on reframing your negative self-beliefs. Once you adopt a positive perspective, your thoughts, emotions, actions, and experiences will follow.

Many people have tried manifestation and swear that it changed their lives. However, it requires consistency, belief in yourself, and hard work. Manifestation is not wishful thinking. You don't just send positive thoughts to the universe and watch your dreams come true. It involves focusing on your goals and making a real effort.

Tesla's Obsession with Three, Six, and Nine

Nikola Tesla was a Serbian-American engineer and inventor. His inventions shaped the world and led to many advancements and innovations in electrical and wireless technology. One of his most intriguing creations is the 369 Code. It is the belief that certain numbers can influence the manifestation process and help people to achieve their goals.

It is a simple method that involves writing your goals three times in the morning, six times during the day, and nine times in the evening. Repeating your desires in this sequence can strengthen your manifestation and align your energy with the universe. So why did Tesla choose the numbers three, six, and nine for his code?

Tesla held the numbers three, six, and nine in very high regard. Some say he was obsessed with them. He found these numbers intriguing from early childhood. They often appeared in his dreams, leading him to believe they were messages from the universe. He discovered their significance when he was studying circles. He noticed that everything came back as three, six, or nine. He said in an interview, *"If you only knew the magnificence of the 3, 6, and 9, then you would have a key to the universe."*

He studied their spiritual and mathematical significance, concluding that they were the foundation of the universe and existed in every aspect of life.

Tesla's obsession with these numbers manifested throughout his life. He insisted on staying in a hotel room whose number was divisible by three and changed hotels when a room was unavailable. He walked three times around a block before entering a building and cleaned his dishes and utensils with 18 napkins (divisible by three, six, and nine).

The 369 Method has become very popular in recent years, and many incorporate it into their manifestation routine. It is easy and people who have tried it noticed their lives transform.

The Numerological Significance of Three, Six, and Nine

Three, six, and nine are not ordinary numbers. They are mystical and powerful and hold divine and spiritual significance. The number three represents creativity, connecting to the divine, self-expression, the universe's role in the manifestation process, and the relationship between the spirit, mind, and body. Tesla believed that three holds all creation's secrets.

The number six reflects harmony and inner strength that drives you to face and overcome challenges. It is associated with unity and balance, which Tesla believed are significant aspects of the universe. It aligns your power with the universe's natural rhythms and brings stability during manifestation.

Number nine's energy is the essence of 369. It represents compassion, spiritual enlightenment, the finishing line, and the attainment of goals. It also symbolizes renewal, rebirth, new beginnings, transformation, letting go of a past that no longer serves you, and embracing a new and exciting future. Tesla found nine to be the most intriguing number because it held all the positive and negative attributes of all the other numbers.

When three, six, and nine are used together, they can empower your manifestation.

The numbers have been influential in many cultures throughout history. The Latins have a popular phrase, "Omne Trium Perfectum," meaning "Every set of three is complete."

Many cultures consider the number three to be divine. In Celtic mythology, it stood for the three domains (the sky, sea, and land) and the three realms (the physical world, the spiritual realm, and the underworld). In Christianity, it symbolizes the Holy Trinity (Father, Son, and Holy Ghost). Triangles represent stability and are incorporated in many architectural designs worldwide. Tesla believed the number three to be associated with the trifecta (vibration, frequency, and energy) that held the universe's keys. The number six is also present in many shapes, whether natural or man-made, such as the hexagon and honeycombs.

In spirituality, 369 is a musical number that symbolizes spiritual awakening. If you keep seeing this number, it is a sign from the universe that you are on the path to self-discovery.

Tesla's Code Connection to Universal Laws

The 369 code is connected to many universal laws, such as the law of attraction. According to Tesla's theory, the universe operates on the concept that positive thinking attracts positive experiences while negative thinking attracts negative experiences. For instance, you have a job interview and keep telling yourself you are not good enough and will not get the job. These negative statements can affect your thought pattern and make you question your own abilities. During the interview, you become consumed with self-doubt and end up getting rejected.

On the other hand, you wake up one day smiling and telling yourself that today will be a great day. Surprisingly, you receive an acceptance email for the job you applied for weeks ago, and your friend calls you to tell you they have won two spa invitations and want you to join them. You end up having a great day, just like you manifested.

What you put into the world returns to you, so always manifest positive and happy thoughts.

The 369 law is also connected to energy vibrations. Tesla believed that numbers play a universal role that goes beyond mathematics. They hold the secret to understanding energy flow. Everything in the universe vibrates at a different frequency. Upon studying this vibration, Tesla noticed the connection between manifestation and numbers.

He believed people could align themselves with the universe's energy and make their dreams a reality by tapping into these vibrations. Tesla created the 369 Method based on his theory about vibration, frequency, and energy to have a powerful manifestation method that can connect your intentions with the frequency of the universe.

Scientific and Spiritual Intersection

Tesla's spiritual beliefs are backed by scientific research. He regarded the universe as a large energy field and believed in the Hindu concept of "Prana," a Sanskrit word meaning vital energy or life force. Prana is believed to flow through all living beings and impacts their mental, physical, and emotional well-being. Tesla studied Eastern culture and believed that Prana represents the construction of matter and the source of existence. Prana, or the universe's energy, is the force you should align yourself with to bring creativity, strength, and abundance into your life.

Many scientists and physicists have also studied Prana. Austrian physicist Erwin Schrödinger researched the concept and linked it to quantum mechanics. In his paper, he compared it to quantum coherence, the behavior of subatomic particles. He claimed that the life force that flows in all living beings resembles the energy governing the behavior of subatomic particles.

American physicist David Bohm also argued that Prana could explain many aspects of quantum mechanics and prove that all living beings are connected. Indian physicist Amit Goswami agreed with his fellow scientists about the similarities between the life force and the energy flowing in the subatomic particles. He also argued that Prana is linked to quantum physics and consciousness.

All these studies prove that the gap between science and spirituality has become smaller. The 369 method is not a trend but a credible method, as Tesla and many other scientists have proven the validity of spirituality and the universe's energy.

Historical Influence and Modern Adaptations

Modern thinkers owe their ideas to Nikola Tesla's innovation. He was a visionary ahead of his time, and many physicists and scientists followed in his footsteps. While many people only associate him with electricity, Tesla's genius is greater than anyone could imagine. He envisioned a world similar to the one that exists today. Tesla believed that technology would take over and people would rely on it in every aspect of their lives. He also knew that wireless communication and wireless energy transmission were a possibility.

Tesla saw a future that was not limited to the inventions of his era. He was a true innovator who understood what the coming generations needed and how he could make their lives easier. His ideas laid the foundation for many modern-day inventions, such as radar and radio waves, and he even created a concept similar to the Internet.

His inventions and the ideas he could not fulfill are lessons in innovation. Tesla did not just work on improving current inventions *but imagined things that did not exist* and made them a reality.

Tesla's influence goes beyond his technological vision. His spiritual ideas have also been adapted into modern manifestation techniques. People use his 369 Code by writing down their affirmations three times in the morning, six times in the afternoon, and nine times in the evening to strengthen their manifestation and make their dreams come true.

How to Use the 369 Method
1. Set intentions.
2. Create personalized affirmations related to your goals.
3. Visualize making your dreams a reality.
4. Make sure you practice the 369 method every day to amplify your manifestation.

Your thoughts create your reality. You experience different thoughts throughout the day, some positive and some negative. Although you may not pay much attention to them, they can impact your life. You are constantly sending out vibes to the universe without realizing it and may be creating a reality that is different from what you want.

Adapting the 369 Method to your life will help you attract positive experiences. You'll learn to align your thoughts and intentions with the universe's energy to attract what you deserve.

Chapter 2: Start with Setting Intentions

Setting intentions is crucial for any type of spiritual work. It is the first step toward aligning your thoughts and energy with the universe. Intentions are powerful. They can keep you focused on your goals and prepare you for what the universe has in store for you. However, some people don't know how to set intentions properly and usually just repeat general statements that don't reflect what they really want.

Setting intentions is the foundation of spiritual work.[2]

This chapter explains the concept of intention-setting, helps you find your passion in life, provides strategies for crafting effective intentions, and explains the role of repetition in manifestation. You will also discover common mistakes people make when setting intentions.

Understanding Intention-Setting

Intentions reflect how you want to experience life. They are the dreams and visions you want to manifest and make into a reality. They are different from resolutions, which lack flexibility and can be demanding. Intentions are a soft voice from the deepest part of your soul that guides you toward transformation and growth.

Intention-setting is recognizing your desires, putting them into words, and releasing them to the universe. This technique encourages you to identify and affirm your inner strength. It invites you to ask yourself tough questions such as, "How do I want to impact the world and the people in my life?" "What qualities do I wish I had?" Answering these questions is the first step toward setting intentions and staying true to your authentic self.

Setting intentions is one of the most significant parts of manifestation. It transforms your thoughts and desires into tangible reality. Intentions give your thoughts a purpose and drive you toward focusing your energy on manifesting your goals. Setting intentions and taking action to make them a reality creates a deep bond between you and the universe.

Your intentions can change over time. As you grow and evolve, you start to want different things out of life. For instance, you may have wanted to travel the world a few years ago or go on fun adventures with your friends. Now, you may want a successful career and financial stability. Intentions are not set in stone. You can always change or redefine them to fit your current vision.

Intention-setting is essential to activate the 369-manifestation method. You cannot manifest your goals without first declaring what you want to achieve to the universe.

Aligning your emotions with intentions can change your mindset from negative and passive to positive and proactive, guiding your decisions and actions toward the life you envision. This mindset can make you believe in yourself and your abilities, strengthening the impact of your intentions.

Benefits of Intention-Setting

- Intention-setting allows you to live mindfully. When you are aware of your intentions, you become focused on the present and make decisions that align with your vision.
- Your actions become aligned with your goals.
- Your mindset shifts, and you start enjoying the journey instead of worrying about the destination.
- Intention-setting requires you to look within and discover your passions and goals, leading to self-discovery and personal development.

Examples of Intention-Setting

- I intend to connect with nature
- I intend to tap into my creativity
- I intend to love my body
- I intend to practice self-care
- I intend to let go of the past

Pinpointing Your Desires

Setting intentions can be challenging if you are uncertain about your goals. However, these simple techniques can help you pinpoint your desires, find your passion, and manifest your dreams.

Meditation

Meditation allows you to self-reflect and find what you are destined to do with your life.

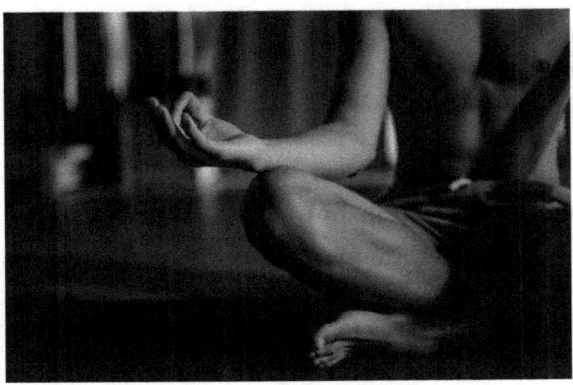

Meditation.'

Instructions:
1. Find a quiet room and remove all distractions.
2. Lie down or sit in a comfortable position.
3. Close your eyes and take a few long, deep breaths to clear your mind and relax your body.
4. As you inhale, visualize your feet or body connecting to the earth below you. Visualize the earth breathing into your body. The air enters your feet and then goes through your thighs, belly, back, and into your heart.
5. You become more grounded in the present moment with every breath you take.
6. Don't think of anything except this moment.
7. Exhale and visualize the earth releasing all your tension, worries, stress, and negative energy from your body. You will feel lighter, more present, and more grounded with every breath.
8. Inhale and feel a sense of calm and peace fill every part of you. Exhale and let go of anything that makes you feel heavy.
9. Your connection to the earth makes you feel relaxed, nurtured, whole, and safe.
10. Only focus on this moment and your present self.
11. You are now connected to the divine energy of the universe and your higher self. Ask them any question you want to ask.
12. What have you been focused on lately? Is there something that has caught your attention recently? Are there certain thoughts or themes that keep arising? What is your authentic self trying to show you?
13. Is there something you have always wanted to do but couldn't due to limited resources, time, money, or fear of failure or rejection? Is there something holding you back from exploring your passions?
14. What do you find inspiring? What do you enjoy doing?
15. If nothing is holding you back, what do you imagine yourself doing? Answer this question without considering your limiting beliefs, self-doubt, and other people's judgment or approval.
16. What did you enjoy doing as a child? What were you good at?

17. What do you know in your heart that you believe to be true? Perhaps you have a belief about yourself that you have been avoiding. Maybe you want to explore new horizons or want to make an impact on the world. Whatever you decide to do with your life, know that the universe will support and guide you.
18. Are you willing to take risks and leave your comfort zone to try something new?
19. What is your next step? What do you want to do to get closer to the life you envision? What can you do or change to align with your most authentic self?
20. Visualize warm golden light surrounding you. You can see now what you should do. Trust yourself and the universe's wisdom.
21. Refocus on your breathing. Slowly open your eyes and bring your awareness to your surroundings.
22. Write the answers to all these questions in your journal and reflect on them.

Exploration

Get out of your comfort zone and explore new hobbies and interests. You may find something you enjoy. Learn something new in your free time to broaden your horizons. You can join a community group, read a book, take an online class, or attend workshops.

Accept Your Mistakes

It is normal to make mistakes when exploring and trying new things. Don't be hard on yourself. Mistakes provide a learning opportunity, so reflect on what they can teach you, make adjustments, and try again. Continue with this trial-and-error process until you find something you enjoy. Avoid negative thoughts such as "I am a failure" or "I am not good enough." Explore your passions with a positive attitude and a clear mind.

Ask for Advice

Ask your family members, friends, or mentors to guide you to find your passion. They may be older and have more experience than you or may have encountered a similar situation. Engage in conversations and discussions until something sparks your imagination.

Commit to Your Passion

Once you find your passion, commit to it. Learn more about it, challenge yourself, and grow. Dedicate time to explore and nurture your new interests to boost your self-confidence.

Set Goals

After uncovering your passion, the next step is setting goals.

- Write down your goals and hang them on a wall or a vision board to easily track them. This can strengthen your intentions and motivate you to work hard to accomplish them.
- Divide big goals into small ones to make them more manageable and less overwhelming. Achieving each of these small goals will give you a sense of accomplishment and motivate you to keep going.
- Reward yourself each time you finish a goal on time or before the deadline. Buy yourself a small gift, or take yourself out for dinner.
- Use the SMART method to organize your goals and make them attainable.
    - **Specific:** Make sure your goals are specific to your current needs and align with your plans.
    - **Measurable:** Decide how you'll evaluate or measure your progress. Doing this shows you if you are moving forward or falling behind and need to change or adjust your plan.
    - **Achievable:** You should have the skills, time, and resources to accomplish your goals.
    - **Realistic:** Your goals should be attainable so you can achieve them. Unrealistic goals will waste your time, frustrate you, and lower your self-esteem.
    - **Time-Bound:** Set a reasonable deadline for your goal that allows you time to work on it while keeping you focused to prevent procrastination and delays.

Steps to Crafting Effective Intentions

You need to set clear and straightforward intentions to use with the 369 Method.

Reflect

Take time to self-reflect and decide what you want. Taking this break provides you with the clarity you need to set clear and specific intentions. Try journaling or meditation to find what you want to achieve or what will make you happy. Focus on your core beliefs and values to set intentions that align with your true self and long-term goals.

Focus on Yourself

Focus only on yourself and your goals and dreams. This is your journey and you are the only one who can choose the destination. Don't concern yourself with other people's opinions or judgments. However, this can be challenging. Nowadays, most people are obsessed with how others perceive them. Instagram is filled with manipulated pictures to create fake images of people solely to impress others.

Consider this an opportunity to train yourself not to be concerned about how others think and only focus on what you want. Remember, you are the only one who will reap the benefits of your choices or suffer the consequences.

Don't Focus on the "How"

You don't need a plan to set your intentions or have everything figured out from the start. That will come later. First, you should send your intentions to the universe and trust that it will guide you.

Believe in the Universe

Once you set and utter your intentions, believe that the universe has received them and is working for you. That does not mean that you should sit and do nothing. You should still try and do the work while believing you'll succeed because the universe has a plan for you. You should also listen to your intuition because this is how the universe guides or sends you messages.

Write Your Intentions

Writing down your intentions and hanging them around the house will reinforce them, make them more tangible, and amplify your manifestation. Put them in places where you'll constantly see them, such as your home office or bathroom mirror.

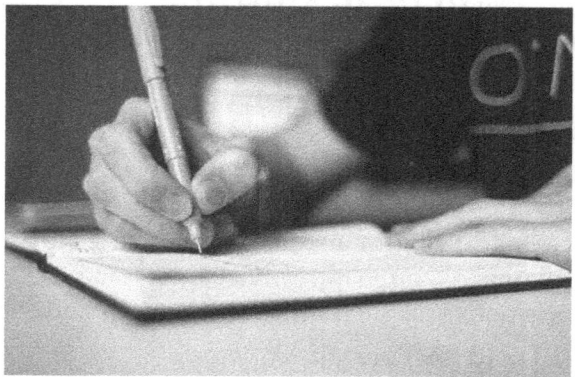

Write down your intentions.'

You should also use the present tense when writing, as it will change your mindset into believing that your intention is already happening. Avoid negative statements and only focus on what you want to invite into your life. For instance, instead of saying, "I don't want to be alone," say, "I feel loved."

Take Action

Setting intentions is merely the first step. You should take action to make them into your reality. Break them down into small steps and work on them daily until you manifest your dreams.

Common Mistakes People Make When Setting Intentions

Some people claim that intentions don't work. However, they may be making mistakes that prevent the universe from manifesting their intentions.

Vague Wording

The most common mistake people make when setting intentions is using general and vague statements. This is similar to walking in the desert without a compass. You'll keep moving around without reaching a destination.

Your intentions should be straightforward and clear. For instance, instead of saying, "I want more money," say, "I want a $5000 raise this year." Before you set an intention, you should know exactly what you want so you can use the correct wording.

Using Negativity

When you set intentions, you should send out to the universe what you want, not what you do not want. Avoid negative words and a pessimistic mindset. Positive thoughts and statements can make you believe in yourself and open your heart and mind to many possibilities. Don't focus on thoughts such as "I am not good enough" and focus on ones that highlight your abilities, such as "I am smart and capable and will get the promotion I deserve."

Focusing Only on Your Current Options

You may find yourself in a bad situation, such as a toxic relationship or a deadened job. This can make you feel stuck with no hope of things changing. Your negative thoughts have made you blind to any new opportunity that comes your way. You believe that you'll never be free and will be unhappy forever. This defeated mindset can bring more negativity. You cannot set intentions when you don't believe your situation will improve.

Challenge these thoughts with visualization techniques to help you envision a better future.

Self-Doubt

Self-doubt is the enemy of positive thought. You cannot set an intention if you don't believe in yourself. You'll also send a negative frequency to the universe that could impact the outcome of your manifestation. For instance, how can you set an intention that you want to have a successful career if you keep thinking of your past failures? You need to reframe your thoughts and believe you are worthy of success and can achieve your goals.

Impatience

People expect to see results right after they set intentions. If this does not happen, they become frustrated and question if manifestation or the 369 code works. However, setting intentions is not magic. Your manifestation can take months or even years to become a reality. You should understand that everything takes time, so be patient and persistent. Don't stop setting intentions; believe the universe is preparing something amazing for you.

Power of Repetition and Focus

Repetition amplifies intention. Imagine talking to a friend and saying something once, but you are unsure if they heard you, so you say it again. While the universe will always hear and receive your messages, repeating intentions allows your words to send stronger frequencies that echo through the universe, increasing your chances of transforming your dreams into reality.

By repeating your intentions, you'll always be focused on them. They will constantly be on your mind, driving you to work harder to make them tangible. Repetition also shifts your mindset. Instead of worrying about the challenges you may face, you focus your energy on the goal itself and how your life will transform once it's manifested.

How to Write Your First Intentions

Use the strategies in this chapter to create three specific and positively framed intentions related to love, money, or healing.

Intentions are more than just words you repeat during manifestation. They are powerful messages you send to the universe to let it know you are ready to receive everything you deserve. Make intentions part of your daily routine and communicate your thoughts to the universe daily. Use specific and positive statements and believe in yourself.

Chapter 3: Manifesting Love with 369

Love is the most profound feeling in the world. This four-letter word turns people into poets and gives songs meaning. Everyone wants to be loved and longs for companionship. Whether platonic or romantic love, nothing is better than having people who support and care about you. However, love and relationships can be complicated, and you may need help to improve and strengthen your relationships.

Love is the most profound feeling in the world, and you can manifest it.[5]

This chapter defines love manifestation, provides techniques to create a positive mindset, and offers visualization exercises and affirmations to use with the 369 Method to improve the power of your manifestation.

Defining Love Manifestation

Love manifestation is aligning your emotions, thoughts, and actions to attract love. This concept suggests that you can find love when you are confident, content, and fulfilled instead of searching for love to fill a void in your life. You manifest love by attracting the energy you release to the universe.

With these simple steps, you can use the 369-manifestation method to attract romantic, platonic, or self-love.

1. Think of a feeling you want to attract, such as, "I love myself" or "I am worthy of love."
2. Write down the intention three times in the morning.
3. Then, write it down six times in the afternoon.
4. Finally, write it down nine times at night.
5. Repeat every day.

Preparing Your Mindset and Space

You need to create a positive mental and physical environment for manifesting love. Positivity attracts warm and loving energy. By sending to the universe positive vibrations, you are letting it know that you are prepared to receive all that it has to offer. These techniques can prepare you and put you in this state of mind.

Visualization Exercise #1

This exercise can relax your body and bring peace of mind to prepare your mindset for the manifestation of love.

Instructions:

1. Find a quiet, comfortable place with no distractions, like your bedroom or backyard.
2. Lie down or sit in a comfortable position.
3. Close your eyes and take long, deep breaths for one to two minutes or until completely relaxed.
4. Visualize a place where you feel relaxed, safe, and authentic. This place can be a real one that holds a special meaning to you, such as your grandmother's house, a natural spot like the beach or a waterfall, or an imaginary place.

5. Make your visualization vivid by envisioning every detail and engaging all your senses. For instance, if you visualize the beach, engage your eyesight by looking at the blue sky and the beautiful ocean. Feel the air as it brushes through your hair and the warm sun on your skin. Listen to the sound of the waves and take in the beach's smell.
6. Notice how comfortable you feel in this place. You are relaxed, safe, and at peace. Let these feelings wash over you, releasing your stress, anxiety, and tension.
7. Surrender to the feelings you are experiencing now. If you want to cry, cry. If you want to smile, smile.
8. Stay in this place for as long as you want. If your mind wanders, refocus and bring it back to your visualization.
9. After you have finished, return to reality by moving your fingers and toes, taking deep breaths, and slowly opening your eyes.

Loving Kindness Meditation Visualization

This exercise brings you love and self-compassion and can prepare you for self-love manifestation.

Instructions:
1. Find a quiet place where you will not be disturbed.
2. Sit in a comfortable position and relax your body.
3. Close your eyes and take long and deep breaths.
4. Visualize that you are in perfect health and experiencing emotional and mental wellness.
5. Imagine feeling love and compassion for yourself.
6. Express your gratitude for the person you have become.
7. Believe that you are perfect just the way you are.
8. Feel the peacefulness wash over you.
9. Take a long, deep breath and imagine you are inhaling love and compassion.
10. Exhale and release all the tension and negative emotions that hold you back.
11. Repeat affirmations while breathing, such as, "I am healthy and strong," "I am safe and at peace," or "I am loved."

12. Stay in this state for a few minutes. If your mind wanders, bring it back to these feelings of self-compassion and love.
13. Imagine all these positive feelings enveloping you.
14. Visualize you are sitting with someone close to you, such as your child, parent, spouse, or best friend.
15. Hold them and express your love and gratitude to them.
16. Stay with this feeling for a few minutes.
17. Imagine you are sitting with your other family members and friends. Visualize each one of them happy and in perfect health.
18. Envision your acquaintances, coworkers, neighbors, and extended family members.
19. Extend to them feelings of compassion, gratitude, kindness, and love.
20. After you have finished, open your eyes and feel the joy of all the love you shared with the people in your life.

Powerful Affirmations for Love

Affirmations are short statements with powerful words that challenge your negative thoughts and help you cultivate a positive mindset. Repeat affirmations daily with the 369 Method by writing your favorite affirmations three times in the morning, six times in the afternoon, and nine times at night.

- I am deserving of deep and fulfilling love.
- Love flows to me effortlessly and abundantly.
- I am inviting love into my life.
- I deserve a loving relationship.
- I am grateful for the compliments I receive.
- I am intelligent, interesting, and unique.
- I am open to finding true love.
- I am worthy of the compliments I receive.
- My heart is open to giving and receiving love.
- I attract trusting relationships.
- The universe is bringing me all the resources I need to find my soulmate.

- My ideal partner is coming to me.
- My positivity attracts love.
- I am manifesting my soulmate.
- I release anything that stands in the way of finding true love.
- I deserve love and respect.
- I am enough.
- I radiate positivity, beauty, and love.
- My self-love attracts love.
- I trust myself and my choices.
- I am confident in myself and my abilities.
- I have learned from my mistakes. I forgive myself and am moving on.
- I embrace my self-growth.
- I am grateful for my family and friends' love.
- I prioritize my health and well-being.
- I am at peace with who I am becoming.
- I am a beacon of love and positive energy.
- I feel loved and supported.
- I honor my emotions and self-expression.
- I am constantly growing and evolving.
- I celebrate my inner strengths and positive qualities.
- I treat myself with compassion, kindness, and respect.
- I am creating a space in my life for a healthy relationship.
- I manifest the love I want.
- I trust that the universe will bring me the love I deserve.
- I manifest supportive and fulfilling relationships.
- I create joy in my life.
- I attract a relationship that is aligned with my desires.
- I am manifesting an empowering career.
- I am attracting a partner who matches my personality.

- I am attracting abundance into my life.
- I am a magnet for health and happiness.
- I focus on the positive aspects of my relationships.
- I am committed to building a healthy and strong relationship.
- I set healthy boundaries in my relationships.
- I feel safe to be myself.
- I prioritize self-care.
- I am patient and kind to my loved ones.
- I treat others with empathy.
- I see the good in others.
- I practice self-compassion.
- I am surrounded by love.
- I enjoy spending time with my family.
- I am grateful for my family and friends.
- My family cares about me and my needs.
- My family and friends understand me.
- I am grateful to be a part of my family.
- I love my family, and they love me unconditionally.
- I feel safe to be myself around my family and friends.
- My family is my support system.
- I can rely on my friends.
- I am an honest and loyal friend.
- I attract long-lasting friendships.
- I am blessed to have understanding friends.
- I am a great listener.
- My friends make me laugh.
- All my friends are amazing in their own way.
- I value the commitment I share with my partner.
- I am grateful for my accomplishments.
- I am safe and secure in my relationships.

- The love I seek also seeks me.
- I make time for my loved ones.
- I am fulfilled.
- The universe is guiding me to love.
- I am open to all types of love.
- I send love, and I receive love.
- I am intelligent, interesting, and unique.
- I am grateful knowing love will find me.
- I let go of my past and prepared to find love.
- I love to give and receive.
- The more love I give, the more I receive.
- I am worthy of respect.
- I am grateful for the love and receive.
- Real love begins with me.
- My heart is open.
- The universe has wonderful things in store for me.
- I have so much to share with the people in life.
- I choose happiness every day.
- I can overcome any obstacle I face.
- I can achieve all my goals.
- I am not perfect, but I am constantly improving and growing.
- I am working on becoming the best version of myself.
- I am proud of my accomplishments.
- I belong here.
- I matter.
- I am good.
- I am talented and smart.
- I am generous and kind.
- I am brave and strong.
- I trust my choices.

- I am at peace with my past and mistakes.
- I accept my flaws and imperfections.
- I am grateful for my body.
- I am beautiful inside and out.
- I respect myself.

Visualization and Emotional Connection

Visualization is a powerful and effective tool for manifesting love. However, this technique goes beyond closing your eyes and imagining different scenarios. Visualizing love should be vivid and real. You should feel the emotions as if they are already happening to boost the power of your manifestation.

Use these tips to make your visualization more vivid.

Engage All Your Senses

Engage all your senses when visualizing. For instance, imagine yourself on a date with your soulmate. Visualize what you are both wearing, every detail about the restaurant, the smell of your coffee and their perfume, the taste of your food, the texture of your clothes on your body, the sound of soft music from a distance, and how you feel when you are with them. Add as many details as you can to make your visualization feel real.

Feel the Emotion

Don't just visualize love, but feel it. Imagine yourself in love with butterflies in your stomach and the excitement of a new romance. With platonic love, feel the closeness and emotional connection when you visualize your family or friends. Even in self-love, you should experience self-compassion, self-esteem, and joy.

Practice Everyday

Like any skill, visualization needs practice. Spend a few minutes each day visualizing to train your brain to create realistic and vivid images. Immerse yourself in the experience, and you will notice improvement over time.

Now that you have learned how to make your visualization real, it is time to try these techniques to attract all types of love into your life.

Self-Love Visualization

No one is worthy of your love more than you. Practice this exercise and learn to love the person that matters most. You can also practice this exercise to connect with a loved one emotionally. Follow the same steps, but envision the other person, your spouse, best friend, or a family member.

Instructions:

1. Find a quiet place with no distractions.
2. Lie down or sit in a comfortable position and close your eyes.
3. Release the tension from your body by practicing neck and shoulder rolls.
4. Take deep breaths through your nostrils and exhale through your mouth.
5. Scan every part of your body, from the crown of your head to your toes.
6. If you feel any tension, take slow and deep breaths to release it.
7. When you reach the heart, fill it with love and gratitude for its kindness, compassion, and strength during tough times.
8. If you experience distracting thoughts, acknowledge them and let them pass without judgment.
9. After scanning your body, take a few deep breaths before you start the visualization.
10. Envision any place where you feel calm and safe such as your childhood home, park, the forest, or by a lake.
11. Once you choose a place, make your visualization vivid to engage your five senses. Add details to make the place seem real.
12. Let the feelings of calmness and serenity wash over you.
13. Walk around the place you visualize.
14. As you explore the place, you see someone sitting on a bench or a couch.
15. You go and sit next to them.
16. They are looking down, so you cannot see their face, but you feel connected to them.

17. None of you says a word but you can feel they are unhappy and unloved.
18. This person looks up, and you realize that it is you.
19. You look into their eyes and experience everything they are feeling.
20. You realize that your other self needs reassurance.
21. You tell them about all their amazing qualities, remind them of all the adversities they have overcome, and list all the goals they have achieved.
22. Notice how you feel when you say these beautiful things to your other self in this peaceful place.
23. Keep sharing your feelings with them.
24. Hold their hand while looking into their eyes and their soul.
25. Take three deep breaths. Inhale everything that you are and exhale the things you are not.
26. Give your other self a big hug and whisper in their ears, "I love myself."
27. Now, you are ready to leave your other self. Tell them that you will always be here for them to remind them of their importance.
28. As you say goodbye and walk away, think of the love you have shared with them.
29. Take one last look at them and notice how happy and confident they look.
30. Take three deep breaths and slowly open your eyes.

Love Story

Manifest love by acting as if you have already found it. Imagine that you have found the love of your life, and write your love story in detail. Include all the necessary information, such as what they look like, how you met them, how you realized they were the one, etc. Be detailed and write as if you have lived this experience. Visualize everything you write.

For instance, "*I can't believe my partner and I have been together for three years. I still remember the first time we met. It was on December 23, two days before Christmas. I went to visit my family but ended up meeting my soulmate. They were my cousin's friends and spent Christmas with us because they couldn't fly home on the holidays. I remember the first moment I saw them. I was wearing a Christmas sweater and my favorite blue jeans. They were wearing a long black coat and pants covered in snow. My cousin introduced us, and we both smiled at each other. They were wearing gloves, but took them off to shake my hands. When our eyes met, we both felt something. We were standing by the fireplace, and there were sparkles in our eyes. I still remember how their blue eyes pierced my soul, and I couldn't stop smiling."*

This is an example of how detailed your story should be. Continue writing until you reach the future you envision for yourself and your soulmate. You can get married and have kids or travel the world together. You can take a sentence or two from your story, such as, *"I am so grateful that I have finally met the love of my life. I don't think I have ever been happier,"* and write it down three times in the morning, six times in the afternoon, and nine times at night. Do this for 33 days to amplify your manifestation.

Practical Exercises

Morning Affirmations for Love
Write love-focused affirmations three times each morning. Example: "I attract kind and supportive love into my life."

Midday Affirmation Repetition
Repeat your chosen love affirmations six times in the afternoon to reinforce your intention.

Evening Visualization Routine
Before bed, write your affirmations nine times and spend a few minutes visualizing that you are surrounded by love, feeling grateful and joyful.

Who doesn't want to love and to be loved? This is the only emotion that governs everyone. You can manifest this powerful feeling to find a romantic partner, strengthen relationships with your family and friends, and learn to love yourself. Use visualization to prepare yourself mentally for manifesting love. Practice affirmations every day while applying the 369 Method to amplify it. Manifest love as if you have already found it and believe you will one day.

Chapter 4: Using 369 for Money, Abundance, and Success

Do you want to be successful and have more money? While manifestation isn't a magical solution, it can help you find wealth and career success by aligning your thoughts with prosperity to unlock the flow of abundance. This chapter explores how you can overcome limiting beliefs and shift your mindset to invite positivity into your life. You'll also discover effective visualization techniques and powerful affirmations with the 369 Method.

All of us want abundance and success.[6]

Overcoming Limiting Beliefs

Money is essential, yet it is a taboo topic that most people are uncomfortable discussing. Many would rather engage in conversations about sex or race than about their wealth or money trouble. As a result, they don't talk about their limited beliefs concerning money. Some believe they are destined to live paycheck to paycheck and will never be able to save money or achieve their dreams. Others believe their passion or dream job will never bring them financial stability.

You must let go of your limiting beliefs to be rich and successful. Do you think people like Bill Gates or Steve Jobs questioned their abilities to be wealthy? These thoughts prevent you from achieving your goals and can make your affirmations and intentions less effective.

You should learn to recognize and reframe these negative beliefs and replace them with positive thoughts that can lead you to success.

It Is Hard to Make Money

This is one of the most common limited beliefs people have about money. If your family had money troubles growing up, you may believe everyone is destined to struggle financially. As a result, you may not pursue high-paying jobs or ask for a raise at work because you don't think you deserve it. You may also feel that you have no control over your income. Your boss decides your salary, and it is up to clients to buy from your business.

Challenge these thoughts by repeating powerful affirmations that can change your mindset, such as, "*Money comes into my life easily and joyfully.*" You need to believe that you are in control of your financial situation. This belief can motivate you to take action to increase your income and lead the lifestyle you have always wanted.

You Will Never Be Able to Save Money

Many people find that their income only covers their expenses, and they don't have extra to spare. Even if their income increases, they always feel it is not enough. This leads to the limited belief that you'll never be able to save money and achieve any of your financial goals.

However, you can change your perspective from "*I can't save money*" to "*I can manage my spending so I can have more to spare.*" This shift in perception shows that saving money simply requires changing your relationship with it.

You Can't Make Money Doing Something You Love

Many people were raised to believe there is a difference between their passion and career. You have probably heard statements like, "*You can love to paint or sing, but you'll never make money from these hobbies.*" This limiting and discouraging belief can create mindsets that believe creativity isn't going to benefit them.

You can reframe this thought by saying, "*My passion can bring me profit*" or "*I can make money doing what I love.*" Passion leads to innovation and enthusiasm. You'll also be more focused and eager to work hard when you do something you love.

You Don't Deserve to Have a Lot of Money

Low self-esteem can lead you to believe you don't deserve money or success. Perhaps you don't have the skills and abilities to improve your financial status. Self-love and financial affirmation can help you to increase your confidence and perspectives. Tell yourself, "*I deserve money and success,*" or "*I have what it takes to be rich and successful.*"

Money Doesn't Buy Happiness

Some people do not try to make more money because they think it doesn't buy happiness. While happiness can't be bought, money can provide financial security and resources to make your life easier and more comfortable. For instance, if you have enough money, you can afford to take a few days off and go on a vacation to relax and unwind. This belief has discouraged some people from trying to make more money or pursue wealth.

Money is essential and can provide you and your family with better healthcare, schools, etc. Reframe this thought: "*Money can provide me with options to create a good life for myself and my family.*"

Money Is the Root of All Evil

You will hear this common statement if you say you want to manifest wealth. It can discourage you from elevating your financial status and lead to fear of being rich and successful.

Money is a tool, and people can use it for good or evil. Selfish and greedy individuals will spend their money differently from caring and generous ones. Don't let these thoughts hold you back. Remind yourself of what you can do with money such as giving to charity or helping someone in need. Replace these limiting thoughts about money with, "*Money allows me to help others and be a better person.*"

More Tips on Overcoming Limiting Beliefs

- Understand that limiting beliefs are not facts. You can overcome negative thoughts by reframing your mindset and using positive language when you think about your skills or finances.
- Challenge these beliefs by treating them as criminals. Interrogate them and try to find evidence to support them. Negative thoughts are usually based on facts, so challenging them will be easy.
- Adopt a more realistic and positive belief.
- Use affirmations with the 369 Method to challenge and contradict the negative thoughts and help you adopt a positive mindset.

Aligning with Abundance

Manifesting abundance requires you to shift your mindset to align with its energy.

What Does Abundance and Success Mean to You?

Abundance means something different to each person. Before you align yourself with its energy, you should define what it means to you. You cannot get into this mindset if you don't know what you want. Ask yourself, what would an abundant life look like? How would it feel to be abundant? Write down your answers and reflect on them.

You should also decide what success means to you. Do you want to be financially successful and have a fulfilling career? Or do you want to focus on your family and raising happy and healthy children?

Embrace Change

You cannot escape change. It is inevitable. Embrace it and consider it an opportunity for growing and learning.

Practice Gratitude

Reflect on yourself and your life, and practice gratitude every day. Notice all your blessings, such as a successful career or a loving family. Recognizing all the wonderful things you have can alter your perspective and open your eyes to the abundance in your life.

A simple strategy for practicing gratitude is to wake up early every morning to reflect on all the good things in your life.

- Wake up early and reflect on the positive things in your life to start your day at a slower pace.
- Shift your thoughts to focus on the positive. For instance, you wake up with back pain. Instead of focusing on that, be grateful for having a roof over your head and a warm bed that you can sleep on every night. This can give you an energy boost to get you through the day.
- Make a list of all the things that make this day special, such as having a fantastic job, a loving relationship, a comfortable car, etc.

Live in the Moment

Practice mindfulness techniques such as meditation, breathing exercises, journaling, or nature walks to help you live in the moment instead of dwelling on your past mistakes or worrying about the future. These exercises will anchor you in the present whenever your thoughts wander, giving you a sense of abundance.

Celebrate Others

People with an abundant mindset can be happy for others and celebrate their accomplishments. This fosters a sense of community and love instead of competition. You should also learn to appreciate others and make it a habit to notice their positive qualities before their negative ones. This will teach your brain to think of people positively instead of criticizing them. You should also meet people with a smile and compliment them.

Affirmations for Financial Success

Use these affirmations with the 369 Method:

- I attract unlimited wealth and opportunities.
- Money flows to me easily and effortlessly.
- I am building my wealth.
- I am letting go of my limiting beliefs about money.
- I have a healthy relationship with money.
- I use my wealth to help others.
- My prosperity is limitless.
- I am financially empowered.

- My life is filled with wealth.
- I am confident in my financial strategies.
- I manifest financial peace and stability.
- My actions lead to prosperity.
- I deserve my wealth.
- I enjoy my money.
- I have what it takes to earn more money
- My financial situation is improving.
- I am open to receiving wealth from the universe.
- Money will always come my way.
- I will always find ways to increase my income.
- I deserve to make more money.
- I accept and receive prosperity.
- I deserve and accept the abundance coming my way.
- My life is filled with abundance, prosperity, and wealth.
- I can be prosperous and successful.
- It is acceptable to want more money.
- I am committed to living my dream life.
- I can achieve my financial goals.
- I can overcome many troubles that stand in my way.
- Wealth is a key part of my life.
- I am worthy of having everything I want.
- I am in charge of my earning potential.
- Good things are coming my way.
- Money doesn't define my worth.
- I am financially secure.
- I have the wisdom to manage my wealth.
- I am financially independent.
- I am powerful and capable of manifesting unthinkable amounts of money.

- My life is filled with opportunities.
- I enjoy living life abundantly on my own terms.
- I give abundantly and receive abundantly.
- I am on my way to becoming wealthy.
- I always attract money and success.
- I am grateful for all the abundance coming my way.
- All of my dreams are manifesting.
- I am limitless.
- My life is aligned with my purpose.
- I have plenty of space to expand in all areas of my life.
- I invest in myself and my future.
- Money flows into my life.
- I can afford to live my dream life.
- Money often comes to me in wonderful and unexpected ways.
- I know that what is mine is waiting for me.
- I am surrounded by opportunities to make more money.
- I'm amazed by how rapidly I have enhanced my financial wealth.
- I can overcome the fear of money.
- Everything I give returns to me.
- My financial potential is endless.

Visualization for Prosperity

Manifestation involves living your life as if you have already achieved your goals. Practice visualization and imagine yourself living your desired life with abundant wealth and opportunities.

Instructions:
1. Find a quiet room with no distractions.
2. Sit on a chair in a comfortable position or lie down.
3. Relax your jaw if it is tight.
4. Uncross your legs and sit up straight.

5. Feel the sensation of the bed or chair below you.
6. Close your eyes and focus on your breathing.
7. Take a deep breath and feel the air filling your lungs.
8. Exhale and feel the air as it exits your body.
9. Put one hand on your stomach and feel it as it rises and falls with every breath.
10. Keep breathing until you feel completely relaxed
11. Inhale comfort and calmness.
12. Exhale all the tension and stress in your body.
13. Feel a sense of peacefulness wash over you.
14. Inhale and count to three.
15. Exhale and count to five.
16. Repeat three times.
17. Let your breath take you into a deeper state of relaxation.
18. In this calm state, believe in yourself and your ability to change your views about money.
19. Open your mind to allow yourself a unique perspective on the role money has in your life.
20. This new perspective will put you on the path of wealth and prosperity.
21. Self-reflect and find the persistence and determination within to make smart decisions and take action to increase your income.
22. Visualize yourself being successful and living the life you have always wanted.
23. You are happy, secure, and financially abundant.
24. Picture yourself financially secure, traveling the world, and buying everything you want.
25. You have enough money to help others and give back to the world.
26. Envision yourself helping your loved ones and anyone in need.
27. You don't need to have a plan now or know how you will make your wealth. Believe that you'll find inspiration and unlock your potential to take the right steps.

28. Believe that your inner wisdom will guide you.
29. Your new mindset allows you to make better choices and decisions and increase your wealth.
30. You listen to your gut because you trust your instincts and are confident enough to ask for advice when you need it to make more money.
31. You are in charge of your own actions and know which path to take to make a difference in the world.
32. Remain in this peaceful state of mind and visualize yourself sitting by a pond.
33. You can feel the warm sun on your skin, and the cool breeze brushes through your hair. You can hear birds singing in the trees.
34. You notice the water is moving gently in the pond.
35. Leaves are falling into the pond. You put your money-limited beliefs into the leaves and watch them drift away.
36. On one leaf, your money worries float away. On another, your doubt that you'll never be successful or wealthy floats away. Put all your financial concerns into the leaves and let them go.
37. They all drift into the pond and disappear. Out of sight, out of mind.
38. You are free from the negativity and limited beliefs. Nothing holds you back now.
39. Take in the new sense of confidence or abundance.
40. You are now happy and free.
41. You are confident that you'll make money and use it responsibly.
42. You no longer have money worries because you are calm and certain you'll always have more than enough.
43. Inhale to the count of three and exhale to the count of five.
44. You are now feeling lighter as you let go of your worries and negativity.
45. Take three deep breaths. Inhale from your nostrils and exhale through your mouth. Slowly open your eyes.

Practical Exercises

Morning Intention Writing for Abundance:
Write your abundance-focused intention three times each morning. Example: "I am attracting wealth and success into my life."

Afternoon Affirmation Repetition for Financial Growth
Write your chosen abundance affirmations six times in the afternoon to reinforce your mindset.

Evening Visualization and Intention Writing for Wealth
Write your financial intentions nine times before bed and visualize yourself already enjoying the fruits of your success and feeling grateful.

Believe in yourself. You are smart and persistent and can become financially successful. Manifest your financial success by acting like you have already achieved your goals. Let go of your limiting beliefs, reframe your thoughts, align yourself with abundant energy, and work hard while believing that the universe will put you on the right path.

Chapter 5: 369 for Emotional and Physical Well-Being

Did you know you can manifest good health and emotional well-being? While seeing a doctor if you are suffering from any disease is crucial, manifestation can help bring healing, balance, and inner peace. This chapter introduces methods to release negative emotions, affirmations to improve your well-being, visualization for a vibrant body, and holistic healing techniques that can be used with the 369 Method.

Manifest your emotional and physical well-being.[7]

Manifesting Healing and Well-Being with 369

If you experience negative thoughts, you will struggle to align your energy with emotional healing. Before manifesting, you should acknowledge the negativity and its impact on your mental and physical health. You should then practice the 369 Method, which will shift these negative thoughts and feelings and put you on a path of hope, healing, and positivity. Repeating affirmation three times in the morning, six times in the afternoon, and nine times before bed can transform your thoughts and improve your emotional well-being.

A healthy body requires a clear and centered mind. It will motivate you to take action by working out, eating healthily, and practicing self-care. You'll notice your physical health improving when you care for your mental and emotional health.

Filling your mind and heart with positivity can facilitate manifesting physical healing. Commitment to the 369 methods and visualizing a vibrant body can improve your health and well-being.

Mental resilience and peace are necessary for physical and mental healing and overall well-being. Resilient individuals can overcome adversity and find healthy coping mechanisms to deal with their trauma instead of allowing it to define them. This quality can protect you from anxiety, depression, and other mental health conditions.

The 369 Method can help you cultivate resilience and a peaceful mindset by allowing you to focus on the positive, find your strength, and let go of limiting beliefs that make you question your abilities. Affirmations such as *"I am resilient and unstoppable"* can empower you to believe in yourself and your abilities.

Affirmations for Mental and Physical Wellness

- My body is a temple of health and vitality.
- I prioritize my mental health and nourish it with love.
- I care and honor my body and its needs.
- I cultivate positive thoughts and peace every day.
- I invite joy into my life.
- I am calm, centered, and at peace.
- I choose happiness every day.

- I am in perfect health and harmony.
- Every breath I take makes me calmer.
- I am grateful for my good health, vibrant body, and well-being.
- I deserve emotional well-being and mental peace.
- My health improves every day.
- I let go of what no longer serves me to make space for all the wonderful things that await me.
- Healing energy permeates my body.
- I find solace within myself.
- Every cell of my body radiates love.
- I overcome adversity with grace.
- I deserve mental and physical wellness.
- I embrace happiness and positivity.
- My body and mind are strong and vital.
- I always bounce back to good health.
- I am a vessel of peace.
- My soul and mind nurture my body.
- My thoughts, words, and actions reflect the tranquility within.
- I deserve good health and a happy life.
- I only allow empowering thoughts that nurture my mental health.
- I release the stress, tension, and anxiety that prevent my body from healing.
- I am constantly growing and evolving.
- I am grateful for the healing energy flowing through me.
- I release all my worries, and I trust the universe.
- I listen to my body and give it what it needs.
- I gain serenity and mental clarity with every breath.
- Every breath I take rejuvenates me.
- I release past hurt and embrace a future filled with joy and potential.

- I inhale healing energy and exhale pain and discomfort.
- My mind is focused, clear, and calm.
- My body is a vessel of love and well-being.
- I am bigger than my negative thoughts.
- I attract healing energy that constantly restores my body.
- I am committed to leading a healthy life.
- My intuition guides me to make good decisions for my health and well-being.
- My body, mind, and soul are in harmony.
- I nourish my mind with wisdom and knowledge.
- I think kind and compassionate thoughts about my body.
- I cultivate adaptability and mental resilience.
- I embrace rest and give my body breaks when it needs it.
- Healing is a process. I am gentle and patient with myself.
- I nourish my body with healthy food and positive thoughts.
- I release mental clutter and embrace clarity.
- I am grateful for my body's ability to heal.
- My body is a temple; I nourish it with love and compassion.
- I treat my body with kindness and respect.
- I manifest vibrant health in every cell of my body.
- I accept my body and am proud of the journey it has taken.
- My body and mind are in harmony and working together to improve my physical health.
- I make healthy choices that improve my well-being.
- I embrace physical activities and the benefits they bring me.
- I prioritize self-care.
- I invest in improving my health and well-being.
- I connect with my body through self-care.
- I let go of the guilt and forgive myself.
- Taking care of my body empowers me.

- I set an inattention to taking care of my body's needs every day.
- I am grateful every day that my body and mind are healthy.
- I attract experiences that improve my physical and mental well-being.
- I constantly honor the miracle of my body.
- I start each day with positivity and gratitude.

Visualization for Health and Vitality

Practice visualization and imagine a vibrant body full of energy and a positive and balanced emotional state.

Healing Visualization #1
Instructions:

1. Find a quiet place with no distractions and sit in a comfortable position.
2. Close your eyes and take long and deep breaths until you feel completely relaxed.
3. Notice if there is any tension in your body and breathe through it to relax your muscles.
4. Clear your mind and prepare yourself to enter a state of visualization.
5. Imagine a warm, soothing light surrounding you and enveloping you in healing energy.
6. Feel the light as it passes through your body, bringing you healing, restoration, and comfort.
7. Bring your attention to the body parts that require healing, such as discomfort, an illness, or an old injury.
8. Imagine these parts are bathed in healing and soothing light, filling you with warmth and vitality.
9. Take long, deep breaths and visualize the healing light entering the affected parts, soothing any inflammation or pain. It repairs your body by relieving pain in sore muscles, restoring the damaged tissues, and bringing balance to it.
10. Feel your healing energy amplify with every breath you take. It is gently healing your body, and you can feel your pain fading away. You are feeling better than you have ever felt.

11. You can feel your body becoming more vibrant, healthier, and stronger with every breath you take.
12. Allow the healing energy to continue flowing through your body and repeat healing affirmations such as, "My body can heal itself. Healing energy is enveloping me, filling me with its healing power."
13. Spend a few minutes enjoying this feeling of comfort. Your body is no longer ailing or in pain. It is regenerating.
14. Express your gratitude for your body's strength and endurance.
15. After you have finished, slowly open your eyes and bring your attention to the present moment.

Healing Visualization Technique #2
Instructions:
1. Find a quiet place with no distractions, indoor or outdoor.
2. Sit on a couch, chair, or the edge of your bed. Don't lie down. Your feet should be planted firmly on the ground.
3. Sit up straight but not so much to avoid straining your back. If you experience back pain, use support or lean back while keeping your feet on the ground.
4. Close your eyes and take long, deep breaths.
5. Relax your forehead, eyes, neck, and shoulders.
6. Breathe normally but slowly and gently.
7. Keep breathing until you feel relaxed.
8. Visualize a waterfall or rain falling.
9. Engage all your senses. Listen to the rain fall on the ground, watch the beautiful view of the cloudy sky, smell the rain, taste it with your tongue, and feel it on your skin.
10. The image should be realistic and clear.
11. Visualize yourself standing under the rain. Feel the water as it falls on your back, neck, shoulders, and head. Each drop runs down your thighs, calves, and feet.
12. Imagine the water drops washing away all the pain, tension, or discomfort you feel in your body.

13. Repeat this image of the rain washing away your physical pain in your head three or four times.
14. You now feel lighter and more energetic as the pain has been washed away from your body.
15. Take three deep breaths and slowly open your eyes.

Pain Relief Visualization
Instructions:
1. Sit in a quiet place with no distractions.
2. Close your and take a few long, deep breaths.
3. Scan your body for discomfort or pain from the top of your head to your toes.
4. Visualize any pain you are feeling as a red ball. It can be any size you want. You can change the shape and color of the ball to represent your pain.
5. You will see the ball moving further away from your body every time you exhale.
6. Repeat the exercise and notice how you feel each time you exhale, and the mental image of your pain keeps moving further away.
7. You can also imagine the shape crumbling, disappearing, exploding, or using any method that helps you visualize the main leaving your body.
8. Now that the pain has left your body, visualize how you feel physically, mentally, and emotionally. Picture your body feeling healthy and vital.

Emotional Release Visualization
Instructions:
1. Find a quiet room with no distractions.
2. Sit in a comfortable position or lie down.
3. Take a few deep breaths to clear your head.
4. Visualize yourself in a beautiful and mysterious forest. Engage all your senses.
5. Listen to the sounds of the insects and the birds singing on trees.

6. Feel the earth below your feet and the dead leaves crunching with every step you take.
7. Smell the fresh air as it brushes through your hair.
8. Watch the beautiful trees and the animals running around the forest.
9. You see someone sitting on a bench from a distance. You come closer and see that it is your teenage self.
10. Sit next to your teenage self and ask them how they are feeling.
11. Acknowledge your feelings and ask your teenage self if anything is troubling them and how you can help.
12. Learn about their hopes and dreams and what you can do to make them a reality.
13. Connect with your teenage self and learn about their needs and what can make them happy.
14. While talking with your teenage self, you notice a bird flying towards you.
15. It holds a gift in its beak for you. Imagine this gift represents what your teenage self needs to achieve their goals, such as self-belief, persistence, high self-esteem, ambition, etc.
16. Unwrap this gift and observe the form it takes.
17. Give it to your teenage self. Now, you have what it takes to achieve your young self's dreams.
18. Take a moment to reflect on how you feel after empowering your teenage self.
19. Now, visualize yourself on a cloud. You see a child playing; they are your inner child.
20. They feel confident, comfortable, happy, and relaxed.
21. Engage your senses. Listen to your clothes flapping in the wind, feel the wind on your skin, take in your surroundings, and smell the fresh air in the sky.
22. Approach your inner child and ask how you are feeling, what your dreams are, and what you need to achieve them.
23. Find if anything is troubling your inner child and what you can do to help them feel better.

24. Spend a few minutes connecting with your inner child and reflecting on your childhood to find what they need to be happy.
25. You look up and see an angel holding a gift and flying towards your inner child.
26. Let your inner child choose the gift. Imagine what your inner child wants based on your understanding of their needs.
27. Allow your inner child to open the gift and notice how they feel when they see it.
28. Now, visualize yourself looking back on the past. You can see your inner child and your teenage self, who are now enjoying the gifts you gave them.
29. Imagine these gifts had colors. What would they be? Now, imagine they made a sound. What would it be?
30. Visualize the color and sound entering your body.
31. Now, visualize your inner child and teenage self standing before you. Let them let go of all the negative thoughts and emotions that prevent them from achieving their dreams.
32. Look at your stream of time, release all the negative emotions you have experienced in your life, and replace them with the colors and sounds of the gifts.
33. You have now released all the negative emotions you have been carrying since childhood and replaced them with positivity and hope. You are now happy and free from the burden of the past and have all the skills and abilities you need to achieve your goals.
34. Take three long, deep breaths, open your eyes, and return to reality.

Holistic Healing

Holistic healing is a wellness approach that focuses on your emotions, spirit, mind, and body to improve your well-being. According to this approach, every part of you depends on the other. If one part does not work properly, the rest will suffer. For instance, if you suffer from anxiety, your physical, emotional, and spiritual health will be affected. You may experience insomnia, headaches, fatigue, chest pain, indigestion, dizziness, rapid breathing, and rapid heart rate. It may also cause withdrawal, isolation, self-sabotage, negative thoughts, constant worrying, feeling lost, and inability to connect with one's intuition.

A holistic approach can bring balance to every aspect of yourself to protect your overall health. It involves meditation, breathing exercises, massage, yoga, hypnosis, acupuncture, and cognitive behavioral therapy.

You can integrate the 369 Method into the holistic approach. For instance, you can practice meditation three times in the morning, yoga six times in the afternoon, and breathing exercises nine times before bed.

Practical Exercises

Morning Intention Writing for Emotional Balance

Write your intention for emotional healing three times each morning. Example: "I am healing emotionally and embracing inner peace."

Afternoon Affirmation Repetition for Physical Health

Repeat affirmations for physical wellness, such as "My body is strong and full of vitality," six times in the afternoon.

Evening Visualization for Overall Healing

Write your healing intentions nine times before bed, followed by a visualization of your body and emotions being restored to balance and health.

Manifestation is a powerful tool that can make you feel better physically and emotionally. It allows you to invite positive thoughts and emotions into your life, which can relieve your physical pain. Use the 369 Method to heal your body, mind, heart, and spirit and become healthy and strong.

Bonus: 369 Manifestation Routines

This section includes daily, weekly, and monthly strategies you can practice alongside the 369 Method.

Daily Practices

Repeat these affirmations every day following the 369 Method:
- Asking for help is not a weakness.
- I am allowed to ask for what I want.
- I am complete as I am.
- I am optimistic and believe that tomorrow will always be better.
- I don't allow my circumstances to control me.
- I receive the messages the universe sends me.
- I am in charge of my happiness.
- My loved ones always support me.
- I am becoming the best version of myself.
- I don't fight change. I embrace it.
- I don't compare my progress with anyone. I am growing at my own pace.
- I am true to who I am, and I don't pretend to be someone else.

- I treat my body with respect.
- I don't allow anyone to cross my boundaries.
- I am proud of my accomplishments and how far I have come.
- I celebrate other people's success.
- I am in control of my reactions and responses.
- I inhale trust and exhale doubt.
- I invest in myself.
- I forgive myself and set it free.
- Every day is an opportunity for learning and growth.
- I celebrate myself every day.
- I accept and embrace my quirks.
- I am not competing with anyone.
- My heart knows the right path to take.
- I am open to new experiences.
- I embrace new opportunities.
- I am excited for whatever future the universe has for me.
- I want to be happy. I don't chase perfection.
- I let go of my fears and embrace safety and security.
- I am grateful for what I have and excited for what is to come.
- I nourish my body with healthy food and my heart and mind with positivity.
- I make time for self-care every day.
- I let my intuition guide my choices and decisions.
- My life is full of endless possibilities.
- My life is a canvas, and I am an artist.
- I am grateful for everything in my life.
- Every step I take brings me closer to the life I want.
- I embrace my inner strength and trust my instincts.
- I am growing more confident each day.
- I am strong, capable, and ready to face whatever life throws.

- New doors are always opening for me.
- I am a magnet for positivity and good experiences.
- I learn from my mistakes instead of dwelling on them.
- Every day is a fresh start filled with excitement and wonders.
- I am a warrior and ready to face life's battles.
- Every challenge makes me wiser and stronger.
- I am focused on today and living in the moment.
- I live each day with presence and purpose.
- I find beauty in everything around me.
- I choose kindness every day.
- I spread joy wherever I go.
- I am dedicated to personal growth.
- I am ready to receive the wealth the universe offers me.
- I am loveable, loving, and loved.
- I am worthy of my dreams.
- My possibilities are endless.
- I know I can be all that I want to be.
- I manifest perfect health every day.
- Good things are coming to me.
- I am grateful to be alive.

Breathing Exercises

Practice any of these breathing exercises every day to relieve stress and improve your mental health.

Belly Breathing Instructions:

1. Sit on a chair or lie down in a quiet room.
2. Put one hand on your belly and the other on your upper chest.
3. Relax your belly and take a deep breath through your nostrils.
4. Feel the air moving through your nostrils until it reaches your stomach.
5. Feel your stomach below your hand rising as the air fills it.
6. Exhale slowly through your lips and feel your belly under your hand falling.

7. Notice how the hand on your chest remains still.

Box Breathing Instructions:
1. Exhale while counting to four.
2. Count to four before inhaling.
3. Inhale while counting to four.
4. Hold the air in your lungs and count to four.
5. Exhale and repeat.

4-7-8 Breathing Instructions:
1. Sit with your back straight or lie in bed in a quiet room.
2. Place your tongue's tip on the roof of the mouth behind the upper front teeth.
3. Exhale through your mouth, making a "whoosh" sound.
4. Close your mouth with your tongue placed on the roof of the mouth and inhale while counting to four.
5. Hold your breath while counting to seven.
6. Exhale through your mouth while making a "whoosh" sound and counting to eight.

Lion's Breath Instructions:
1. Sit in a comfortable chair, lean forward, and place both hands on your knees.
2. Spread your fingers as wide as possible.
3. Inhale through your nose.
4. Open your mouth and stick out your tongue.
5. Exhale, carrying the breath across the root of your tongue, and make a "Ha" sound from your abdomen.
6. Breathe normally for a few minutes.
7. Repeat this exercise seven times.

Weekly Practices

Practice these exercises once a week using the 369 Method.

Self-Love Meditation Instructions:
1. Find a quiet room with no distractions.
2. Lie down or sit in a comfortable position.

3. Feel the connection between you and the ground below you.
4. Put both hands on your thighs and close your eyes.
5. Focus on your breathing. Breathe normally, and don't try to change the rhythm.
6. Clear your head and only focus on your breathing.
7. Inhale through your nostrils and exhale through your mouth.
8. Focus on your body and notice the tense parts.
9. Inhale slowly into the parts that hold the tension. Feel your body soften and relax.
10. Exhale the tension in your body.
11. You are feeling more relaxed with every breath.
12. Focus on how you are feeling deep down. Are you closed off or emotionally drained? Is your mind wandering off or focused on every breath? Is it relaxed or filled with doubt, negativity, and restlessness?
13. Take a long, slow, and deep breath. Be focused on the present and let your mind relax.
14. You are loved, anchored, and safe.
15. Feel your breathing washing away your negative thoughts and limited beliefs.
16. Exhale and release the emotions and thoughts that no longer serve you.
17. If your mind wanders, bring your attention back to your breathing.
18. Take a long, deep breath and connect with your truest self.
19. Think of a time when you didn't care about being accepted and focused on being your true self. How did this experience make you feel?
20. Think of a time when you were proud of yourself. What did you achieve? How did it make you feel?
21. Take long and deep breaths. Place both hands over your heart and think of moments when you were judged, treated unfairly, or not accepted.
22. Breathe through these feelings and treat them with kindness and compassion.

23. Forgive yourself for forgetting your personal power, allowing other people's opinions to influence you, and letting them tell you how you should feel.
24. Tell yourself, "*I am enough and have always been enough.*"
25. Tell yourself that you must experience pain, challenges, and injustice to grow and find your inner strength. These experiences have taught you to become wiser, kinder, and more compassionate.
26. Inhale and tell yourself, "*I am whole.*"
27. Exhale, release the limited beliefs, replacing them with hope and potential.
28. Inhale and remind yourself of all your amazing qualities.
29. Exhale and release those fears that hold you back, and embrace change and new opportunities.
30. Take slow and deep breaths. Reflect on how you can nurture your soul.
31. Celebrate your creativity and authenticity.
32. Take a deep breath and visualize your heart opening like a rose. Imagine white light pouring into your heart, filling you with self-love.
33. Feel the warm light flowing through your body.
34. Take a few deep breaths, be grateful for the experience, and slowly open your eyes.

Meditation for Manifesting Love Instructions:
1. Sit comfortably or lie down and cross your arms and legs.
2. Close your eyes. Inhale through your nose and exhale through your mouth.
3. Feel the tension and stress released from your body every time you exhale.
4. For the next few minutes, you'll only focus on your breathing.
5. Visualize your perfect partner sitting next to you.
6. Notice their energy. What does it feel like?
7. Feel their presence and the spiritual connection you both share.
8. Feel the love flowing between your hearts. It is a unique connection, and you have never experienced anything like it

before.
9. For the first time, you have no doubts. You know you have finally found the one.
10. Now, start to visualize them. What do they look like? What do they smell like? How does it feel when you are holding hands? Do you feel like you have just met or have known each other all your lives?
11. What does their voice sound like? How do you feel when they speak to you?
12. Imagine you are cooking together, going for a walk, watching movies, or doing any other fun activities.
13. Imagine what your conversations are like. Are you having fun, supporting each other, talking about your future?
14. Be grateful that you have finally found the love of your life. Believe that every experience you had throughout your life led you to this moment.
15. Take three deep breaths and open your eyes.

Monthly Practices

Practice these exercises once a month using the 369 Method.

Self-Reflections Journal Prompts

Self-reflect on your life once a month by asking yourself questions and writing the answers three times in your journal.

1. Who do you trust the most and why?
2. What makes your relationships strong?
3. How do you connect with your loved ones?
4. What do you value most in your relationships?
5. Write down three things you have learned from your previous relationships.
6. Mention five traits you value about yourself.
7. Mention five traits you look for in a partner.
8. How do you show compassion to yourself and others?
9. Mention three things you want to change about your relationships.
10. Do you want to change aspects of yourself? What are they?

11. What boundaries do you want to set in your relationships?
12. What does love mean to you?
13. Mention three things you have always wanted to tell your partner, parents, siblings, or best friend.
14. Does your career fulfill you or leave you wanting more?
15. What part of your job do you enjoy the most?
16. Does your job drain or overwhelm you? Are there aspects of your job you want to change?
17. Does your job offer learning opportunities?
18. What can you improve about your skills?
19. What do you need to accomplish your work goals?
20. Where do you see yourself in five years?
21. When do you trust yourself the most? When do you experience self-doubt?
22. Mention an experience that has changed and shaped you.
23. Finish this sentence, "*My life would be incomplete without...*"
24. Mention three beliefs that shape your personality.
25. Mention three beliefs you are prepared to reconsider.
26. Is there an opinion that you held dear but have recently questioned? What has changed your mind?
27. Describe yourself in five words.
28. Visualize the perfect version of yourself and write five of its traits. What do you need to do to become this person?
29. What are the most important values to you?
30. Are you happy? What do you need to do to be happier?
31. Mention current obstacles you are trying to overcome. Is your strategy working, or do you need to make adjustments?
32. What makes you excited about the future?
33. Do you have time for your favorite hobbies? Why not?
34. Where do you feel most at peace? Describe these places using your five senses.
35. Write a short letter to your past self and another to your future self.
36. What did you look forward to growing up?

37. What parts of life surprised you, and which ones disappointed you?
38. What advice would you give your teenage self?
39. What activities do you enjoy doing when you are sad? Do they make you feel better?
40. If you could relive your life, what would you do differently?

Mindful Walking

Spend an hour mindful walking while enjoying nature's beauty. Reflect on your life and whether what you do with your life aligns with your long-term goals.

Incorporate 369 methods in your daily, weekly, and monthly routine. Find other practices that you enjoy and do them using Tesla's code.

Conclusion

You attract what you believe, and your thoughts can make or break your life. If you think positively, you'll bring love, success, and abundance into your life. Negative thinking, however, will make you doubt your abilities, and you'll be unable to achieve your goals. Nikola Tesla's 369 manifestation code can alter your thought pattern so you can start believing in yourself and chasing your goals.

The book began by explaining Nikola Tesla's obsession with the numbers three, six, and nine, their role in numerology, and their power in spiritual traditions. It also explored how his work connected scientific theories with spiritual concepts, making his theory more credible. You discovered the impact of Tesla's ideas on modern thinking and how the 369 method was adapted to modern-day manifestation techniques.

You understood how intentions can strengthen your manifestation techniques and help you attract positivity. Intentions work best when repeated. You learned the role of focused attention and repetition to amplify your manifestation and help you attain your goals.

The 369 method can help you to find love and strengthen relationships with your family and friends. You discovered how affirmations can be incorporated into Tesla's techniques to change your thoughts and inspire you to believe you are worthy of love. The book provided strategies such as visualization and emotional connection to boost the power of manifestation.

Don't let your inner critic and negative thoughts hold you back. The book introduced techniques to help you overcome limiting beliefs that prevent you from achieving financial success. You also learned to alter your mindset with the energy of the universe to attract abundance.

The book offers affirmations to change your perspective and help you believe you can succeed financially. You also discovered how visualization can help you imagine the life of your dreams, which includes wealth, abundance, and great opportunities.

You learned how the 369 Method can bring you peace, mental resilience, and better physical health. Visualization techniques were provided to help you picture a healthy, energetic body and a positive and well-balanced emotional state. The book provided tips to incorporate holistic healing into the 369 Method to improve your physical, mental, and spiritual health.

The 369 method goes beyond a few techniques you can apply in your free time. It is a way of life, and manifestation should be a part of your routine. Incorporate the exercises in this book into your daily life and make it a habit to set intentions and manifest anything you want.

Part 2: 369 Manifestation Journal

Daily Journaling to Manifest Abundance, Love, Wealth, Emotional Well-being, and Your Heart's Desire

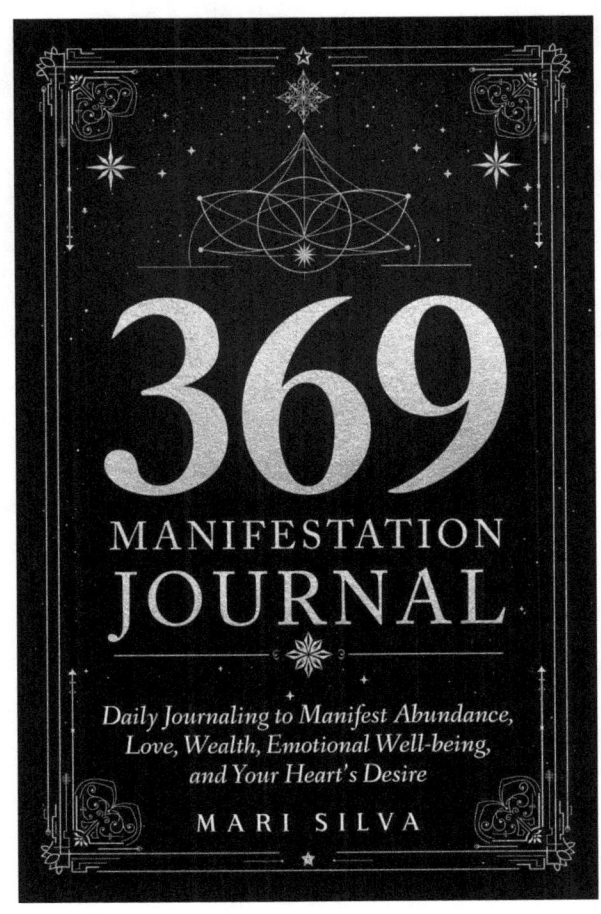

Introduction

Manifestation can help you align your energy and mindset with your goals to live the life you have always wanted. The 369 Method is one of the most popular and effective manifestation strategies. It focuses on practicing affirmations, intentions, and other techniques in a specific sequence to help you achieve your goals.

The book begins by introducing the 369 Method and explains how it can help you manifest your desires. It then describes how you can attract abundance with daily good habits that can transform your life. You will also learn to harness the power of manifestation to invite romantic love and self-love into your life.

The 369 Method can put you on the path to financial success and help you achieve your financial goals. You will also discover the power of intention and learn how it can help you gain clarity and focus your energy on manifestation.

The last chapter focuses on manifesting emotional well-being and inner peace to cultivate a clear and positive mindset. The book includes various exercises and daily rituals that reinforce your manifestation journey. Creating a consistent mindful practice that aligns your thoughts with your goals is key to manifesting your desires.

Your dreams are just a few affirmations away. Begin your journey today and transform your life.

Start Your 369 Practice

Section 1: BEGIN

Life is meaningless without dreams. Every person has some kind of goal they want to reach. Some want to find love, while others want to buy a big house or get a promotion. While some goals are easy to achieve, others can be challenging. Manifestation can bridge the gap between dreams and achievement. However, manifestation isn't a magical solution to all your problems. It is a method that can transform your mindset by replacing negative thoughts with positive ones.

Using the 369 method is an effective manifestation tool.'

The 369 technique is one of the most popular and effective manifestation methods to help you attract your desires. This chapter introduces the method and provides exercises and prompts to help you to manifest your dreams.

The 369 Method

The 369 Method is a manifestation tool for focusing thoughts, bringing intentions to life, and laying the groundwork for future manifestation success. It involves writing your goal three times in the morning, six times in the afternoon, and nine times in the evening. The repetition of this sequence can amplify your intention as you send it out to the universe and align its vibrations with your goals. It also shifts your mindset. Repeating affirmations strengthens your self-confidence, replaces negative thoughts with positive ones, and helps you to develop a successful mindset. The 369 Method includes affirmation, visualization, journaling, and setting intention.

Consistency is key when practicing the 369 Method because it creates a rhythm that aligns with the universe's energy and reinforces your intention in your subconscious mind. Writing your manifestations multiple times makes it a sacred ritual that creates a strong frequency of expectation and belief. Going days without manifestation can disrupt your focus and energy flow.

The method is based on Nikola Tesla's theory that the numbers three, six, and nine are powerful and hold the key to the universe. The numbers also hold significance in the law of attraction and numerology making it one of the most powerful manifestation methods available.

- **Number Three:** This represents manifestation, self-expression, creativity, and your connection with the divine. It also symbolizes the link between the spirit, the mind, and the body.
- **Number Six:** It is associated with harmony, balance, stability, and inner strength. The number can increase your spiritual power and align your energy with that of the universe.
- **Number Nine:** It symbolizes transformation, rebirth, new beginnings, and letting go of the past.

The 369 Technique has gained popularity recently due to its simplicity and power. It does not require much work. You just set an intention for what you want to manifest, creating affirmations in the present tense that align with your desire, such as *"I am grateful for the love that fills my life."* Repeat the affirmation using the 369 Technique and visualize your life as if your dreams have already been manifested.

While manifestation is a powerful tool, it will not work without action. Work hard, take advantage of opportunities, and believe in yourself. Aligning your intention with your actions can strengthen your manifestation.

Prompts and Exercises

These exercises will start you on your manifestation journey. Work on them in the order they are presented below.

1. Write Your Manifestation Statement

Create a clear, concise manifestation statement that reflects your primary goal. The statement must be in the present tense, as though the desire has already been realized. Example: *"I am grateful for attracting abundance into my life."* Write and/or recite this statement three times in the morning, six times at midday, and nine times before bed, following the 369 Method.

_____

_____

_____

Visualization Exercise

Close your eyes and vividly visualize that you have already achieved your goal. Focus on sensory details – what you see, hear, feel, and experience. Make your visualization realistic by including every detail and engaging your five senses. For instance, imagine the colors of the trees, leaves, and flowers if you visualize a forest. Watch the birds in the trees and animals running at a distance. Smell the flowers around you, feel the cool breeze on your skin, and listen to the birds singing and the leaves crushing under your feet. After you have finished, write down what you experienced. If you do not know what to write, these questions can help you.

- Describe everything you saw and everyone you encountered.

_____

_____

_____

- Write down all the sounds you heard.

  _____
  _____
  _____

- What did you feel throughout the visualization?

  _____
  _____
  _____

- Did a person or an animal speak to you? What did they say?

  _____
  _____
  _____

- Did you see something unusual?

  _____
  _____
  _____

- Was there a message from the universe in the visualization? What was it?

  _____
  _____
  _____

- Would you repeat the experience? Why or why not?

  _____
  _____
  _____

2. Create a Daily Ritual for 369 Practice

Set specific times during the day to perform your 369 practices (morning, midday, and night). You should create a calming ritual to accompany your writing, such as lighting a candle, practicing mindful breathing, or meditating for a few minutes. Perform your 369 practices consistently at the same times each day.

Calming Breathing Exercise Instructions:
1. Find a quiet room with no distractions.
2. Lie down or sit in a comfortable position.
3. Close or open your eyes. Choose whatever makes you comfortable.
4. Place one hand on your belly and another on your chest.
5. Take a long, deep breath through your nostrils. Feel the air fill your lungs as your stomach rises below your hands.
6. Breathe out through your mouth and feel your belly fall under your hand. Notice how the hand over your chest does not move as much.
7. Repeat three or four times while focusing on your belly's movement.

Calming Meditation Instructions:
1. Find a quiet room with no distractions.
2. Sit in a comfortable position with your back straight.
3. Breathe at your normal pace.
4. Close your eyes and only focus on your breathing.
5. Feel the air as it enters through your nostrils and fills your body.
6. Notice how the air exits your body through your mouth.
7. You may experience distracting thoughts while meditating. Do not focus on them, resist them, or allow them to distract you.
8. Acknowledge these thoughts without judgment, let them pass, and bring your attention back to your breathing.

3. Gratitude Practice for Manifestation

Practice gratitude before manifestation to boost your mood, reduce stress, and remind yourself of all your blessings. This will help you focus on the good things in your life and put you in the right frame of mind to manifest. When you are focused on the positive, you will believe that more good things can happen to you, reinforcing your intention.

Make it a habit to write in your journal every day about three things you are grateful for, such as your home, family, friends, career, etc. You can also write about small things that happen to you, such as having a good cup of coffee or receiving a loving message from an old friend.

4. Affirmations

- I am grateful for the small steps I take every day.
- I find joy every day.
- I let go of negative thoughts and replace them with positive ones.
- My thoughts are peaceful and calm.
- I treat myself with respect, patience, and kindness.
- I attract positivity wherever I go.
- I am excited about the opportunities I attract.
- I am grateful for my skills and abilities.
- My joy comes from within.
- I find the bright side in every situation.
- I embrace happiness.
- My past does not control my decisions.
- I only allow healthy relationships in my life.
- I manifest joy every day.
- I celebrate my achievements every day.
- I choose to bring joy to others every day.
- I prioritize my health and happiness.
- External factors do not determine my worth.
- I chase passions and interests that make me happy and fulfilled.
- I manifest the life I want.
- I trust my inner voice.
- I make choices that bring me closer to my heart's desire.

5. Check-In Section

Track your manifestation progress by writing down how many times you have manifested.

The 369 Method is a powerful manifestation technique that can alter your mindset to focus on the positives. It aligns your thoughts and energy with your goals to motivate you to take action to make your dreams a reality. Practice manifestation using the 369 sequence daily to remain consistent and attract your heart's desire.

Attract Abundance Daily

Section 2: ABUNDANCE

The 369 Method can help you attract abundance. Affirmations and other manifestation techniques can align your thoughts and actions with an abundance mindset, promoting positive energy, prosperity, and good habits.

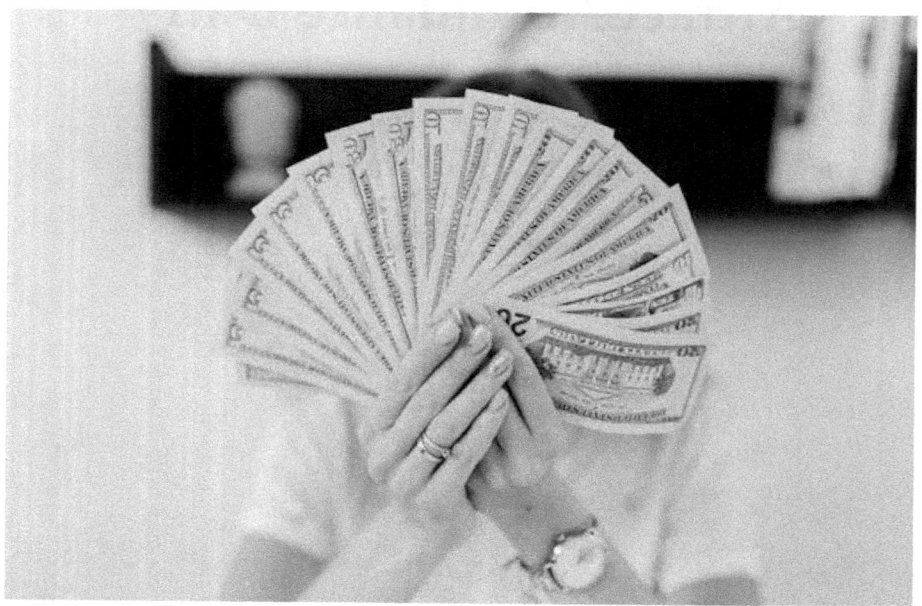

Learn how the 369 method can help you attract abundance.'

This chapter explains the concept of abundance and its impact on your daily life. It also explores the importance of gratitude and affirmations.

Abundance

Abundance is the belief that there is enough success, happiness, and wealth for everyone. Life is filled with opportunities. If one door closes, another will open. This mindset encourages you to be optimistic and to approach life's challenges with a positive attitude. Say you apply for a job and get rejected. Instead of feeling angry or defeated, consider that this was not the right job for you and that a better one will soon come along.

People with an abundance mindset see opportunities instead of challenges. They believe that even the hardest experiences can have positive outcomes. They know there is a lesson, better options, or a chance for growth behind every rejection or break-up. This mindset also encourages them to focus on the positive and appreciate the good things in their lives instead of obsessing over what they do not have. They learn to embrace every opportunity, accept that change is a part of life, and are unafraid to step out of their comfort zone.

Gratitude

Gratitude can alter your mood and transform your daily life. It shifts your attitude and thoughts away from negativity to a positive mindset. You start focusing on the good things in life and overlook the negatives. For instance, you are moving to a new apartment but cannot afford to hire a moving company. Instead of focusing on your money problems, you can focus on how fortunate you are to have a place of your own or siblings or close friends to help you move.

Practicing gratitude releases dopamine and serotonin, which improve your mood. It also reduces stress and anxiety.

The Importance of Gratitude

- **Increases Your Patience:** Expressing gratitude daily can reduce your impulsiveness, boost your self-control, and increase your patience.
- **Helps You Focus on the Positives:** Life can be full of distractions, and it is easy to forget all your blessings. You can also become fixated on the negatives during tough situations. However, practicing gratitude reminds you of all the amazing things in your life, no matter how hard things become. Writing down what you are grateful for will rewire your brain to always look for positive things.

- **Reduces Comparisons:** Practicing gratitude reduces negative self-talk and boosts your self-esteem. As a result, you will not feel the need to compare your life to the lives of others. You will be so happy and satisfied with your life that you will not pay much attention to what you lack.

- **Encourages Mindfulness:** People who practice gratitude do not think about past regrets or worry about the future. They simply focus on the present and appreciate what is happening in their lives. For instance, you have an important meeting next week, but today, you are meeting your best friend for coffee. Instead of worrying about the meeting, you are grateful for spending time with a friend and enjoying a nice drink.

- **Reminds You of What Matters:** When a person loses their job, they may feel that it is the end of the world. However, gratitude reminds you of what matters, such as your health, family, and having great friends. You will always find something to be thankful for, no matter how bad the situation is.

Affirmations

Affirmations are short, positive, and powerful statements that you repeat to yourself to replace negative thoughts with positive ones. These words tap into your subconscious to alter your mindset, challenge you, and motivate you to chase your goals.

The Importance of Affirmations

- **Reduces Stress and Boosts Confidence:** Affirmations build resilience and reduce stress. Repeating positive statements cultivates a positive attitude and makes you stronger. Phrases such as "I am strong and resilient and can handle anything life throws at me" or "I am capable of handling stress" can help you believe in yourself and handle challenging situations.

- **Increases Your Self-Esteem:** Affirmations reinforce positive beliefs about yourself. They challenge negative thoughts, counteract insecurity and self-doubt, and increase confidence. Statements such as "I believe in my abilities" or "I treat myself with kindness and respect" can shift your self-perception and encourage you to believe in yourself.

- **Boosts Your Mood:** Affirmations challenge negative thoughts and reduce stress, improving your mood and life satisfaction.

Gratitude and affirmations alter your mindset and help you focus on the positives. A positive mindset is necessary for setting intentions and for manifestation. You should be confident and optimistic and believe your dreams will become a reality.

Repeating affirmations every day can help instill a routine that aligns your mental focus with abundance.

Prompts and Exercises

1. Daily Gratitude Affirmations

Write down daily affirmations like, *"I am grateful for the abundance flowing into my life each day,"* and *"Every moment, I am surrounded by opportunities for prosperity."* Write/recite these affirmations based on the 369 Method.

1. _____
2. _____
3. _____
4. _____
5. _____
6. _____
7. _____
8. _____
9. _____
10. _____

2. Visualization of Abundance

What does abundance mean to you? Close your eyes and visualize your life filled with abundance. Focus on sensory details – what you see, feel, hear, and experience in moments of prosperity. After visualizing, journal what you envisioned and repeat your chosen affirmation sequence according to the 369 Method.

_____
_____
_____

3. Create an Abundance Board

Create a physical or digital vision board that represents your abundance-related goals. This can include images, words, or symbols that resonate with your desires. Take a few moments three times daily to review the board and recite your affirmations six times, then reflect on how these visuals align with their daily practice.

4. Morning Journaling Pages for Abundance

Cultivate an abundance mindset by writing in your journal every morning things you are grateful for or happy thoughts to start your day on a positive note. These prompts will get you started if you do not know what to write.

- Write down three things you would like to manifest today and mention why.

- What three things can you do to increase your abundance today?

- Write down one goal you would like to achieve today.

- Set an intention for the day.

- What small change can you make today to help increase your sense of abundance?

- Write down what you want more of in your life, such as happiness, love, money, or success.

5. Evening Reflection

Write positive thoughts in your journal before bed to reflect on your day or what you want to achieve in the future.

- What are you grateful for today?

- Mention the people in your life you are grateful for.

- What did you love about yourself today?

- What went well into your life today?

- Mention five things you would do if money was not an issue.

- What makes you feel happy and fulfilled? What can you do to increase those moments in your life?

- Mention something that has affected you today.

- What would you like to manifest in the near future and why?

- What limiting beliefs do you have about abundance that may be holding you back?

6. Write a Letter

Write a letter to your future self to express your gratitude for the abundance mindset you have developed. Describe how you have changed and grown throughout the years – thanks to the abundance you have attracted.

7. Magical Powers

Close your eyes and imagine you have magical powers that you can use to cultivate abundance in one area of your life. Which area would you choose? How would you use your new mindset to improve your life?

_____
_____
_____

8. Limiting Beliefs

Write down three limiting beliefs that prevent you from cultivating an abundant mindset. How do they impact your life? How can you use the 369 Method to challenge these beliefs?

_____
_____
_____

Practice gratitude and affirmations using the 369 Method to attract abundance. Don't allow adversity to discourage you. Believe that opportunities are limitless and that life is filled with second chances. When something does not work out, believe that the universe has a better plan for you, and another opportunity will soon arise.

Invite Love into Your Life

Section 3: LOVE

Everyone is looking for love. They are either seeking romantic love and dreaming of finding their perfect partner, looking within, and trying to cultivate a healthy relationship with themselves, or wanting to nurture their bond with their friends and families. It is human nature to need to connect with others and develop healthy relationships. The 369 Method can help you manifest love through affirmations, meditations, and other exercises.

This chapter explores the connection between self-love, positive energy, and attracting external love. It also highlights the importance of aligning your thoughts and emotions to welcome love into your life.

The Connection Between Self-Love, Positive Energy, and Attracting External Love

Imagine you see two people walking down the street. One is confident, smiling, and radiating positive energy, while the other is frowning, lacking self-esteem, and radiating negativity. Which one would you approach? Most people will find the first person more likable and approachable because they gravitate toward confidence and positivity. Self-love and a positive attitude make you into a magnet for love.

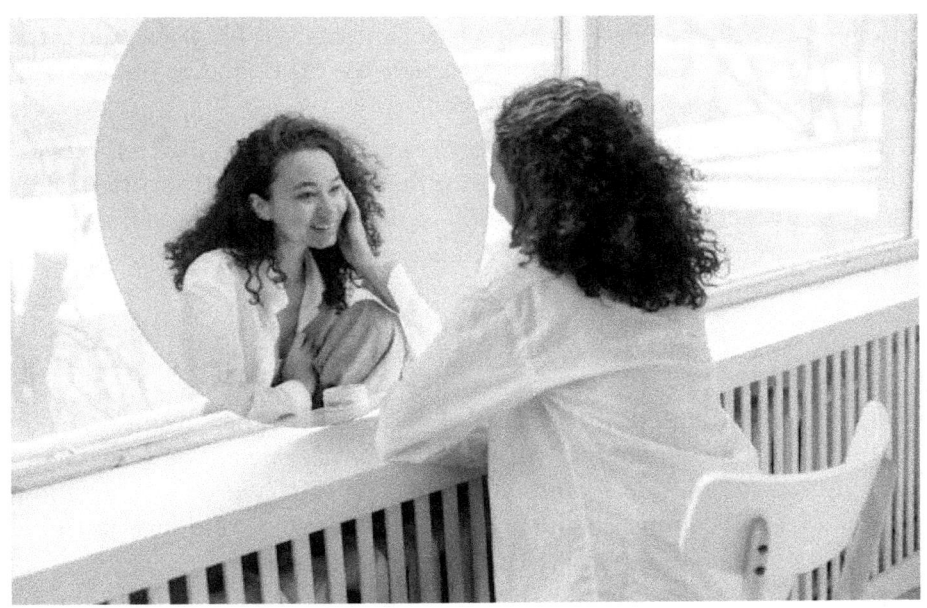

Manifestation starts with self-love.[10]

When you love and accept yourself, you attract positive emotions. People will see your self-love and radiant energy shining outward. You will become a secure, confident, and happy person who knows their worth. These characteristics will help you attract healthy relationships with like-minded individuals.

What you feel inward is reflected outward. You will not attract love if you do not believe that you deserve to be happy or see yourself in a negative light. You will only attract unhealthy relationships with people who do not respect you or treat you in the right way.

Importance of Aligning Your Thoughts and Emotions with Your Goal

Aligning your emotions and thoughts with your goal will motivate you to take action and commit to it. Your energy will be focused on finding love and welcoming it into your life. According to the law of attraction, your thoughts shape your reality. Your beliefs will put you on the right path. For instance, if you believe that you are worthy of love, you will start dating and looking for a healthy relationship. You will not tolerate disrespect or toxic individuals who do not treat you the way you deserve to be treated.

Your thoughts create vibrations or an energy field around you. Positive emotions and thoughts attract positive experiences, such as self-love, romantic love, and platonic love.

The 369 Method focuses on consistency, reinforcing loving intentions, and maintaining a vibration that draws love closer. Repeating a love affirmation following the 369 sequence keeps this emotion in mind and opens you up to what the universe has in store.

Prompts and Exercises

1. Affirmations for Love

Write ten love-focused affirmations that you will repeat using the 369 Method. Examples include: *"I am worthy of deep, unconditional love"* and *"Love flows freely into my life."* Write and/or recite these affirmations three times in the morning, six times at midday, and nine times before going to bed, following the 369 Method.

1. _____
2. _____
3. _____
4. _____
5. _____
6. _____
7. _____
8. _____
9. _____
10. _____

2. Gratitude Practice for Love

Make it a daily habit to write down three things you are grateful for in your relationships or yourself. This will help foster a loving mindset and align your energy with attracting love.

_____
_____
_____

3. Daily Loving-Kindness Ritual

Create a daily self-care ritual, such as a moment of reflection or a loving-kindness mantra. Examples include, *"May I be loved, may I be at peace, may I share love with others."* Repeat this mantra following the 369 pattern, building a sense of inner love.

4. Heart-Opening Visualization

Instructions:

1. Find a quiet room with no distractions.
2. Sit in a comfortable position.
3. Take a long, deep breath, hold it for a few seconds, and exhale with a sigh, emptying all the air in your lungs.
4. Feel your feet grounded by having your feet flat on the ground.
5. Imagine the energy in your heart waking like a cat from its slumber.
6. Visualize your heart waking up in the present.
7. Imagine a golden tube of light flowing out of your heart and moving through your body, leaving a light trail in its path.
8. After the light flows throughout your body, watch it as it slowly and gently exits and disappears into the Earth.
9. You feel your heart and mind relaxing as you watch the light traveling to the Earth's center.
10. You see a crystal-shaped light glowing and radiating peaceful energy from the Earth.
11. It makes you feel calm, centered, and peaceful.
12. It draws your energy to it like a magnet. You watch the golden tube emerge from the Earth, merge with the crystal-shaped light, and become one.
13. You watch both energies together while you breathe slowly. You feel as if time stands still.
14. Take a deep breath of gratitude and feel the energy enveloping you.
15. It is quiet and peaceful. The energy moves slowly through your legs and flows throughout your whole body.
16. You are filled with the Earth's energy now.

17. Breathe slowly and feel yourself sinking into your heart's space.
18. Connect with your heart and set an intention. What does your heart tell you? What does it need to know?
19. Now, feel the combined energy filling it with light.
20. Your heart is bright, golden, and shines like a diamond.
21. The light fills it with grace and love.
22. Visualize the energy flowing through you. Your heart can't contain the energy anymore. It wants to escape.
23. Take a deep breath and open the gates of your heart. You can feel the energy beaming out, shining through you, and spreading like wildfire.
24. As you watch the energy spreading, you see beacons of light shining at a distance. It is the energy of all your loved ones.
25. You see your energy merging with theirs. All the energies are now one and shining brighter than ever before.
26. Your heart is now open to love and inviting others to connect with it. You are ready to love unconditionally.

5. Round-up Journaling Questions

Reflect on your emotional state by answering these journal questions.

- How have you shown love to yourself this week?

_____
_____
_____

- What new loving experiences have happened this week?

_____
_____
_____

- What does your heart need?

_____
_____
_____

- How can you treat yourself with kindness and compassion?

- How can you express yourself authentically?

- Are you at peace with yourself? If not, why not?

- How can you lead a happier life?

- Do you have healthy relationships? If not, what can you do about it?

- Do you need to work harder on your relationships? If yes, what should you do?

- Where do you find inspiration?

- How do you stand up for yourself?

- How can you forgive yourself?

- How can you forgive others?

- Are your thoughts positive or negative?

- How can you strengthen your spiritual connection?

- Do you say "yes" when you should be saying "no"?

- Are there feelings you are holding back?

- What do your spirit, mind, and body need?

- What is your biggest accomplishment?

- Mention five things you love about yourself.

- What makes you different from others?

- Name three flaws you accept about yourself.

- What is standing in the way of loving yourself?

- Why do you believe you deserve happiness?

- What can you do now that your future self will thank you for?
  _____
  _____
  _____

- Mention three things you need to do to practice self-care.
  _____
  _____
  _____

- Write down five things people usually say about you.
  _____
  _____
  _____
  _____
  _____
  _____
  _____

- What makes you feel alive?
  _____
  _____
  _____

- What labels do you use to describe yourself?
  _____
  _____
  _____

- When was the last time you did something nice for someone? What did you do? How did it make you feel?
  _____
  _____
  _____

- Write a thank you letter to yourself.

_____
_____
_____
_____
_____
_____
_____
_____
_____
_____
_____
_____
_____
_____
_____
_____

- What makes you happy?

_____
_____
_____

- What would you want to do with your life if money was not an issue?

_____
_____
_____

- What makes you feel loved?

_____
_____

- Mention three things you love about your body.

  _____
  _____
  _____

- What destructive habits do you want to quit?

  _____
  _____
  _____

- How do you cheer yourself up when you have a bad day?

  _____
  _____
  _____

- Who is your support system? How do they make you feel?

  _____
  _____
  _____

- When was the last time you overcame a challenge? How did you overcome it?

  _____
  _____
  _____

- What does your ideal day look like?

  _____
  _____
  _____

6. Love Check-In log

Log your love manifestation progress in a calendar.

Love is the most beautiful gift that you give to yourself and others. Practice manifestation exercises every day to attract love into your life.

Fuel Financial Success

Section 4: WEALTH

Who does not want to be wealthy? Some people believe that financial success can be challenging. While inflation makes life hard, you can still find ways to save money and improve your financial situation. To do that, you must let go of the limiting beliefs holding you back and embrace a healthy mindset that drives you to act. Manifestation can change your mindset. It will help you to improve your relationship with money, change your spending habits, and make better financial decisions.

Fuel your financial success using the 369 method.[11]

This chapter helps you attract and sustain financial success with consistent practices that align your mindset and energy with your financial goals.

How Mindset, Beliefs, and Visualization Practices Impact Financial Success

Your mindset is directly linked to your financial success. It can either hold you back or push you towards working harder and succeeding. It can also influence your financial decisions and spending habits. A negative mindset will weigh you down and prevent you from taking action, which can negatively impact your relationship with money. As a result, you will struggle with saving and may end up with a huge debt. On the other hand, a positive mindset will be focused on abundance. It will motivate you to pursue your financial goals and manage your money wisely to build your wealth.

Some people have negative beliefs about money, such as the belief that money cannot buy happiness, money is the root of all evil, and you will never be able to save enough money to achieve your goals. These beliefs can prevent you from achieving financial success. However, if you self-reflect, you will realize that these beliefs stem from poor financial habits such as overspending or turning down investment opportunities. This realization can change your mindset and inspire you to change your financial behavior. For instance, you can repeat affirmations to challenge these beliefs, such as, "*I am in control of my spending habits*" or "*I save money to achieve my goals.*"

Visualization is another powerful tool for influencing financial success. Envisioning yourself rich and successful motivates you to act to make these images a reality. Visualization also changes your relationship with money. For instance, if you visualize yourself saving every month, you will start making better financial decisions, such as reducing expenses and setting money aside.

Repeating affirmations using the 369 sequence can help boost your confidence, keep you focused, and attract opportunities to achieve financial success. It will also change how you view money by replacing negative beliefs with positive ones.

You should also support a positive relationship with wealth and money. Your thoughts about money can affect your financial decisions and career choices. For instance, if you think you do not deserve to be rich, you will not ask for a raise at work nor make choices that can improve your financial status.

Many people believe they are not in control of their financial success. For instance, employees feel their bosses determine their salaries, and business owners find that their customers can either make or break their business. However, no one is in control of your financial situation but you. For instance, you can negotiate your salary or find ways to make your product more appealing.

Let go of the defeated mindset that makes you believe there is nothing you can do to be rich. Believe that money and wealth are not impossible to attain. Treat money as a means to help you achieve your goal instead of something that stresses you out or controls your life. Believe that you deserve to be wealthy and happy – and that money will make your life easier and better. Ignore thoughts like, "*Money can't buy happiness,*" as these thoughts can prevent you from achieving your financial goals.

Money can make your life less stressful. If you have enough money, you will not worry about paying rent or supporting your family. You will be able to afford good healthcare and take time off from work when you need to relax and unwind. Once you see money as a tool to improve your life, you will work harder to succeed financially.

Prompts and Exercises

1. Financial Abundance Affirmations

Write daily financial affirmations using the 369 Method, three times in the morning, six at midday, and nine at night). Examples of affirmations: "*Money flows easily into my life*" and "*I am open to new financial opportunities.*"

1. _____
2. _____
3. _____
4. _____
5. _____
6. _____
7. _____

8. _____

9. _____

10. _____

2. Money Block Journaling

This exercise will help you reflect on your beliefs about money. Write responses three times throughout the day using the 369 Method.

- What do you believe about money?

_____
_____
_____

- Are these beliefs helping or hindering you?

_____
_____
_____

- How did your parents' relationship with money influence you?

_____
_____
_____

- Have your limited beliefs about money held you back? What would you do differently if you had a second chance?

_____
_____
_____

- Have societal beliefs about money influenced you?

_____
_____
_____

- What advice would you give to your past self to change their beliefs about money?

_____
_____
_____

- What lessons have you learned from the financial challenges you have faced throughout your life?

  _____
  _____
  _____

- What is your current financial mindset?

  _____
  _____
  _____

- Has your self-worth impacted your financial decisions?

  _____
  _____
  _____

- What beliefs do you have about money that have impacted your identity? (Examples, "I am bad with money" or "I will never be rich").

  _____
  _____
  _____

- How does money make you feel? How do these emotions impact your financial decisions and your relationship with money?

  _____
  _____
  _____

3. Visualization of Financial Success

Close your eyes and imagine a life where financial worries are a thing of the past. Make your visualization vivid by imagining every detail and engaging your five senses – what does your home look like? How do you feel about paying for things comfortably? Include any other sensory experiences. Afterward, write down key aspects of this visualization and repeat the 369 affirmation sequence.

_____
_____
_____

4. Mindful Spending Exercise

Dedicate a part of your day to mindful spending – reflecting on where you spend money and how it aligns with your financial goals. Answer prompts followed by the 369 affirmation practice.

- Does your spending align with your goals?

  _____
  _____
  _____

- What do you usually spend money on?

  _____
  _____
  _____

- Do you waste money or spend it wisely?

  _____
  _____
  _____

- Do you have a budget? Do you stick to it? If you don't, why not?

  _____
  _____
  _____

- When was the last time you bought something you did not need? How did that make you feel?

  _____
  _____
  _____

- Write down your expenses for the last week. What purchases were unnecessary? Is there something you can do without saving money?

  _____
  _____
  _____

5. Wealth Gratitude Journaling

Write down your financial accomplishments daily, big or small, or any steps you have taken that bring you closer to your goals. Express your gratitude for the smart decisions you make or all the resources you have that help you on your journey.

Examples

- I am grateful for my monthly salary, which allows me to take care of my expenses and save for emergencies.
- I am grateful that I do not spend my money on unnecessary things, which allows me to save and achieve my financial goals.
- I am grateful that I am starting to make smart financial decisions that change my relationship with money.
- I am grateful that I cook at home instead of wasting money on takeout.
- I am grateful that I buy my clothes during the sale and save money.

6. Daily Wealth Ritual

Create a personal daily wealth ritual tied to your 369 practice. For example, you could do deep breathing exercises, light a green or gold candle, or hold a coin while reciting your affirmations.

7. Financial Goal Setting Page

Prepare a financial plan that allows you to save money and make better financial decisions. First, you must study your expenses, recognize unnecessary spending, and make cuts to save money. You should also set a budget and make sure to stick to it. Add your other financial goals, such as how much money you want to save in a month or year, what you plan to do with the money, investment ideas, etc.

8. Round-up Questions

- Mention three financial goals you want to achieve today.

_____

_____

_____

- What can you do today to get closer to your financial goals?

　

- Mention three mindful exercises that can keep you aware of your spending habits and help you make smart financial decisions.

　

- What healthy daily habits do you practice that help you achieve your financial goals?

　

- What immediate actions can you take to improve your financial management skills?

　

- What can you do to become more disciplined with money?

　

- What knowledge do you need to become financially successful?

　

- Do the people in your life support your financial goals? What can you do to strengthen your relationship with them?

- What lessons have you learned from past experiences that can help you succeed financially?

　_____
　_____
　_____

- What opportunities are you planning to pursue to improve your finances?

　_____
　_____
　_____

- How will you overcome challenges that prevent you from becoming wealthy?

　_____
　_____
　_____

- How can you cultivate a positive mindset about money?

　_____
　_____
　_____

- How will you prioritize your needs to manage your expenses?

　_____
　_____
　_____

- How will you resist the temptation to avoid spending money on things you don't need?

　_____
　_____
　_____

- Mention advice you have received in the past that can help you achieve your financial goals.

　_____
　_____
　_____

- How will your life change when you achieve your financial goals?

_____
_____
_____

9. Wealth Tracking Log

Track your expenses and savings to see your progress and how close you are to achieving your financial goals.

Do not let anyone tell you that you cannot dream. Success and wealth are possible. People achieve them every day. Believe in yourself, work hard, and manifest your goals to the universe. Change your relationship with money, make smart financial decisions, and make cuts to save money.

Understand that money is not evil or will not make you happy. It is a necessary tool to improve your life and provide you with the necessary resources to achieve your goals.

Manifest Inner Peace

Section 5:
EMOTIONAL WELL-BEING

Everyone wants to live a stress-free life without worrying about other people's opinions or letting daily issues get to them. However, life can sometimes be overwhelming, and you can struggle to stay calm. You may also blame yourself for every mistake or struggle to make peace with some aspects of your life.

A stress free life is what we all aim for.[12]

This chapter explores using the 369 Method to nurture emotional well-being and cultivate inner peace. Using the 369 Method as a daily anchor, you will discover how to align your mindset, promote self-compassion, and center your emotional state.

The Connection Between Emotional Wellness and Manifestation

Manifestation and emotional wellness are connected. Positive emotions and thoughts motivate you to act and achieve your goals. You will also feel empowered and believe in yourself, amplifying your intention and making your manifestation more effective. Manifestation, on the other hand, can improve your emotional wellness. It reduces stress and anxiety by bringing your attention to the positive aspects of your life and distances you from negative thoughts and emotions.

Emotional stability is essential for effective manifestation because it supports clear and positive thinking. Manifestation goes beyond repeating affirmations or visualizing the life you want to live. You should also believe in what you manifest, or it will not happen. For instance, two people repeat affirmations like, "*I deserve success and abundance,*" but one believes what they are saying, and the other does not. Which one do you think will take action to become successful? Emotional stability also keeps you in the right frame of mind to recognize the goals you want to manifest.

The 369 Method and manifestation can help you cultivate a peaceful mindset and enhance self-awareness. For instance, affirmations such as "*I am at peace with my past*" or "*I am smart and strong and can achieve my goals*" will help you cultivate a peaceful attitude and become aware of your strengths and abilities. Journaling and visualization can also keep you calm, reduce your stress, and help you to recognize your true power.

Prompts and Exercises

1. Affirmation Writing for Emotional Balance

Write affirmations promoting inner peace and emotional strength using the 369 Method (three times in the morning, six at midday, and nine at night), such as, "*I am grounded and at peace with myself*" and "*I choose calmness and positivity.*"

1. _____
2. _____
3. _____
4. _____
5. _____
6. _____
7. _____
8. _____
9. _____
10. _____

2. Self-Compassion Ritual

Create a personal self-compassion ritual tied to your 369 daily practice. For example, light a candle or place a hand on your heart while repeating, *"I am worthy of love and understanding,"* three times. Include notes on your experience.

_____
_____
_____

3. Guided Journaling on Releasing Negative Emotions

Answer these questions to identify and release emotional blocks.

- What emotions are you ready to release?

_____
_____
_____

- How do you feel after letting go of negative thoughts?

_____
_____
_____

- What triggered these emotions?

_____
_____
_____

- When was the last time you felt happy and safe? What can you do to feel this way again?

  _____
  _____

- How do you act when you experience negative emotions?

  _____
  _____

- What is your biggest fear?

  _____
  _____

- When was the last time you cried?

  _____
  _____

- How do you express and release negative emotions?

  _____
  _____

- What do you need to let go of to be happier?

  _____
  _____

- What can you do to prevent these emotional blocks?

  _____
  _____

4. Daily Inner Peace Meditation
Instructions:
1. Lie down or sit in a comfortable position.
2. Take a few deep breaths and clear your mind. Focus only on your breathing.
3. Close your eyes and focus on the air entering your nostrils and filling your lungs.
4. Feel the air as it is released through your mouth.
5. Notice how your chest and abdomen feel with every breath you take.
6. Bring your attention to your hands. Open your palms and feel the sensation in your fingertips and fingers.
7. Feel the vibrations from the energy of the universe fill your hands. Take a long, deep breath, and feel the vibrations flowing through your body, bringing you energy of peace.
8. Focus on the center of your forehead and open yourself to the white light of peace.
9. Let the white light wash over your body and fill you with healing energy. It heals every part of you.
10. It releases the tightness in your jaw, softens your eyes, releases the tension in your shoulders, relaxes your tongue and lips, relieves any pain in the abdomen and chest, and relaxes your entire body.
11. Take a deep breath and enjoy the inner peace you are feeling.
12. Focus on the present moment because it is all you have. You do not need to think about the past or worry about the future.
13. Feel completely at peace at this moment.
14. Imagine this peace spreading into every aspect of your life, including your job, relationships, and the places you frequent, such as your home.
15. When you lose touch with your inner peace, bring your awareness to the present moment.
16. Enjoy the quiet and feelings of stillness.

17. When you are ready, bring your attention back to your surroundings.
18. Notice the sounds around you, slowly open your eyes, and stretch your body.

5. Round-up questions

- Mention three things that bring you inner peace.

  _____
  _____
  _____

- What negative emotion, thought, or habit do you need to let go of to cultivate inner peace?

  _____
  _____
  _____

- How can you challenge thoughts that prevent inner peace?

  _____
  _____
  _____

- What calming and comforting words can you tell yourself now?

  _____
  _____
  _____

- What self-care activity can bring you inner peace?

  _____
  _____
  _____

- Does nature bring you inner peace? How?

  _____
  _____
  _____

- Do your relationships bring you inner peace? If not, what can you do to improve them?

- Does your job disturb your peace? If yes, what can you do to change your situation?

- What can you do to spread love and peace?

- What sounds or music make you feel calm and at peace?

- What has inner peace taught you about yourself and the world?

- What habits or physical activities help you cultivate inner peace?

- Which emotions are you trying to avoid? Why?

- What happens when you face these emotions?

- What do you need to cultivate emotional wellness?

6. Emotional Check-In/Tracking Log

Log your inner peace manifestation progress in a calendar.

Inner peace can reduce stress and provide the clarity needed to practice manifestation. Achieve emotional balance by practicing self-compassion and journaling. Remember, manifestation requires a positive mindset and emotions. Practice gratitude, focus on the good things in your life, and repeat affirmations that challenge negative thoughts and invite positive ones.

Conclusion

You can change your life with the power of the 369 Method. Affirmations, intentions, visualizations, and meditations can alter your thought pattern. They can motivate you to believe in yourself and work hard to achieve your goals because you know the universe is on your side. While there are many manifestation methods, the 369 Method has proven effective. It is also simple, and anyone can practice it, even those unfamiliar with manifestation.

The book explained the 369 Method and introduced practices such as visualizations, affirmations, and intentions. You discovered the impact of Tesla's powerful numbers on manifesting abundance with exercises such as gratitude, affirmations, visualization, abundance board, and journaling.

You learned to attract all types of love into your life to nurture long, healthy relationships with prompts and exercises such as loving-kindness rituals and love check-in logs. The 369 Method can also invite financial success into your life. You learned how to attract wealth with manifestation practices such as money block journaling, mindful spending exercise, and daily wealth rituals.

The last chapter focused on manifesting emotional well-being and inner peace with round-up questions and self-compassion rituals. All exercises in the book align your mindset with your desire to bring your dreams to life.

Consistency can amplify your manifestation. Make the 369 practices part of your daily routine to change your mindset and achieve your goals. This book can act as your guide. You can return to it whenever you need ideas on manifestation practices.

If you enjoyed this book, I'd greatly appreciate a review on Amazon because it helps me to create more books that people want. It would mean a lot to hear from you.

To leave a review:
1. Open your camera app.
2. Point your mobile device at the QR code.
3. The review page will appear in your web browser.

Thanks for your support!

Here's another book by Mari Silva that you might like

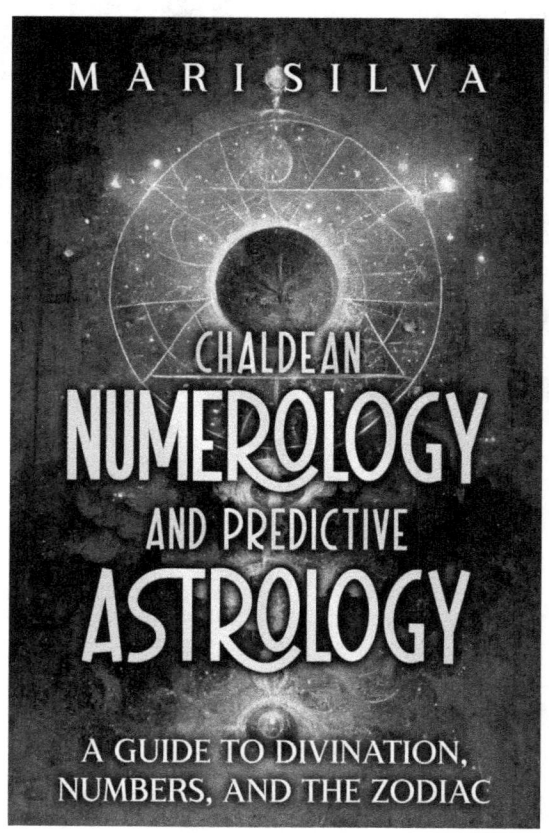

Your Free Gift
(only available for a limited time)

Thanks for getting this book! If you want to learn more about various spirituality topics, then join Mari Silva's community and get a free guided meditation MP3 for awakening your third eye. This guided meditation mp3 is designed to open and strengthen ones third eye so you can experience a higher state of consciousness. Simply visit the link below the image to get started.

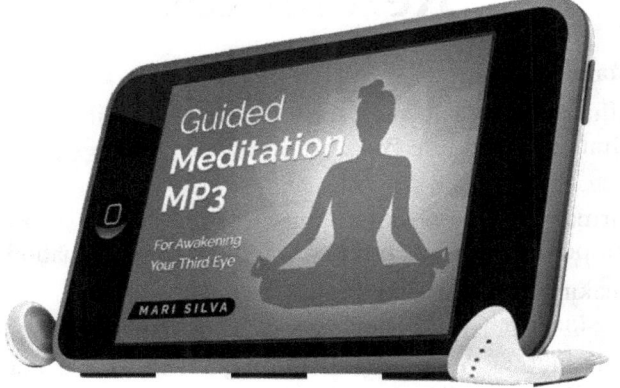

https://spiritualityspot.com/meditation

Or, Scan the QR code!

References

Part 1: 369 Manifestation

110+ Love Affirmations for Relationships, Marriage, Family & Friends. (2022, March 15). Gratitude - the Life Blog. https://blog.gratefulness.me/love-affirmations/

20 money affirmations for a positive mindset. (2022, August 3). Empower. https://www.empower.com/the-currency/life/20-money-affirmations

6 Steps to Breaking Your Limiting Beliefs. (n.d.). PushFar. https://www.pushfar.com/article/6-steps-to-breaking-your-limiting-beliefs/

67 Golden Rules. (2023, August 31). Exploring 369 in Numerology: Spiritual Awakening and Business Alignment. Medium. https://medium.com/@67goldenrules-sg/exploring-369-in-numerology-spiritual-awakening-and-business-alignment-2c36589bd79e

Admin. (2012, September 28). Space is filled with energy - Nikola Tesla - DivineYu. DivineYu. https://divineyu.com/blog/space-is-filled-with-energy-nikola-tesla/

Ali, M. (2023, November 8). Nikola Tesla and Obsession with the numbers 3, 6, and 9. ILLUMINATION. https://medium.com/illumination/nikola-tesla-and-the-numbers-3-6-and-9-abaa61199934

Amara Amaryah. (2024, January 2). 99 Money Affirmations To Attract Abundance Daily. The Good Trade. https://www.thegoodtrade.com/features/money-affirmations/

Ankrom, S. (n.d.). Deep Breathing Exercises to Reduce Anxiety. Verywell Mind. https://www.verywellmind.com/abdominal-breathing-2584115#toc-alternate-nostril-breathing

Batool, N. (2022, July 15). Manifesting Good Health – Don't Just Exist, but Thrive for a Blissful Life! Health & Wellness Blog | Healthwire; Healthwire. https://healthwire.pk/healthcare/how-to-manifest-good-health/#a_healthy_mindset_is_inevitable

Bax, J. (2024). Insight Timer - #1 Free Meditation App for Sleep, Relax & More. Insighttimer.com. https://insighttimer.com/jessebax/guided-meditations/self-love-visualization-meditation

Bell, K. (2024). Insight Timer - #1 Free Meditation App for Sleep, Relax & More. Insighttimer.com. https://insighttimer.com/karenbell/guided-meditations/powerful-guided-meditation-for-attracting-love-manifest-your-perfect-partner-slash-soulmate

Blanchfield, T. (2022, March 24). How to shift from a scarcity mindset to an abundance mindset. Verywell Mind. https://www.verywellmind.com/how-to-shift-from-a-scarcity-mindset-to-an-abundance-mindset-5220862

Branco, D. (2023, September 12). How to Set Clear and Powerful Intentions for Manifestation: The Ultimate Guide. Medium; Medium. https://medium.com/@deborahbranco_55867/how-to-set-clear-and-powerful-intentions-for-manifestation-the-ultimate-guide-9cd579737bdc

Bree. (2024, January 4). The Top 9 Common Mistakes While Manifesting and How to Overcome Them. Gate of Consciousness. https://gateofconsciousness.com/mistakes-while-manifesting/

Brenden. (2023, July 21). Nikola Tesla- A Spiritual Prodigy - Brenden - Medium. Medium. https://medium.com/@brendenford/nikola-tesla-a-spiritual-prodigy-d41f64609e72

Bringle, L. (2020, May 5). Self - 17 Money Affirmations to Attract Financial Abundance to Your Life - Self. Self. https://www.self.inc/blog/money-affirmations

Burdick, E. (2023, October 23). Overcoming the Scarcity Mindness with Abundance. Headspace. https://www.headspace.com/mindfulness/there-will-always-be-more-overcoming-scarcity-mindset

Burris, K. (2024, September 1). The Holistic Counseling Center. The Holistic Counseling Center. https://www.theholisticcounseling.center/blog/anxiety/6-spiritual-symptoms-of-anxiety

Calm Blog. (2024, July 16). Calm Blog. https://www.calm.com/blog/369-manifestation-method

Carroll, L. (2024, January 5). How to Set Intentions and Simplify Your Daily Life. Humble Brands. https://humblebrands.com/blogs/humble-journal/how-to-set-intentions-and-simplify-your-daily-life?srsltid=AfmBOooh-zYufT4OfsbjW1Gkvpt-pq2_PRisElZWT1xHhLDd52Opjq2F cathclaire. (2022, April 29). How to Use the 369 Manifestation Method - cathclaire. Cathclaire. https://www.cathclaire.com/how-to-use-the-369-manifestation-method/

Charters, C. (2021, March 26). Guided Meditation for Self-Worth. The OM Collective. https://theomcollective.org/blogs/meditations/guided-meditation-for-self-empowerment

Charters, C. (2021, March 9). Finding Your Life Purpose Meditation. The OM Collective. https://theomcollective.org/blogs/meditations/finding-your-life-purpose-meditation

Cherney, K. (2023, November 13). Effects of Anxiety on the Body. Healthline; Healthline Media. https://www.healthline.com/health/anxiety/effects-on-body

chillibyte. (2023, January 24). 10 Love Affirmations to Attract a Healthy Relationship. Morale App. https://moraleapp.co/10-love-affirmations-to-attract-a-healthy-relationship/

D'arcy-Sharpe, A.-M. (2020, May 30). Visualization & Guided Imagery for Pain Relief (The Complete Guide) - Pathways. Www.pathways.health. https://www.pathways.health/blog/visualization-guided-imagery-for-pain-relief/

Damon, C. (2021, December 28). 7 Effective Goal Setting Techniques -. AchieveIt. https://www.achieveit.com/resources/blog/7-effective-goal-setting-techniques/

Fraga, K. (2021, August 16). Why Nikola Tesla May Have Thought The Numbers 3, 6, And 9 Hold The "Key To The Universe." All That's Interesting. https://allthatsinteresting.com/nikola-tesla-3-6-9

Global Wealth Hub | Financial Education & Consulting. (2022, December 13). 5 Money Limiting Beliefs that You Need to Overcome ASAP. Www.linkedin.com. https://www.linkedin.com/pulse/5-money-limiting-beliefs-you-need-overcome-asap-global-wealth-hub/

Green, E. (2024, March 17). 67 Positive Morning Affirmation Phrases to Transform Your Day. Starleaf Blog. https://www.starleaf.com/blog/67-positive-morning-affirmation-phrases-to-transform-your-day/

Guide to Manifestation Methods: 369 Method, Positive Affirmations, and More. (2022, June 23). Gratitude - the Life Blog. https://blog.gratefulness.me/369-method-manifestation-methods/

Gupta, S. (2024, March 22). 25 self-love affirmations to remind you of your worth. Verywell Mind. https://www.verywellmind.com/25-self-love-affirmations-8553223

Gupta, S. (n.d.). How to Manifest Your Goals With the 369 Method. Verywell Mind. https://www.verywellmind.com/manifest-your-goals-with-the-369-method-8620625

Health, F. (2024, April 30). Harnessing the Power of Visualization for Healing: The Science Behind its Effectiveness. FND Health. https://www.fndhealth.com/post/harnessing-the-power-of-visualization-for-healing-the-science-behind-its-effectiveness

Ho, T. (2023, January 31). How to Set Intention as Part of Your Spiritual Practice - Museflower Retreat & Spa. Museflower Retreat & Spa. https://musefloweretreat.com/how-to-set-intention-as-part-of-your-spiritual-practice/

Houlis, A. (2021, November 11). 3 Legitimate Ways to Manifest the Kind of Love You Deserve. Shape. https://www.shape.com/lifestyle/sex-and-love/how-to-manifest-love

How to develop an abundance mindset: 8 tips to help you thrive. (n.d.). Calm Blog. https://www.calm.com/blog/abundance-mindset

How To Do The 369 Manifestation Method. (2021, January 7). The Manifestation Collective. https://themanifestationcollective.co/369-manifestation-method/

How to find your passion in life in 5 mindful steps. (n.d.). Calm Blog. https://www.calm.com/blog/how-to-find-your-passion

How To Set Intentions To Manifest Your Dreams In 2024. (2022). Keys Soulcare. https://www.keyssoulcare.com/mind/how-to-set-intentions-to-manifest-your-dreams-in-2024.html?srsltid=AfmBOoq6dhaQSlNtBmYHjhNWil08WmiiDKRc1XTEVvRIpPEeElp-zzL6

HowStuffWorks. (2024, July 25). Unveiling the Profound Significance of Angel Number 888. HowStuffWorks. https://science.howstuffworks.com/science-vs-myth/extrasensory-perceptions/888-angel-number-meaning.htm

Huber, L. (2018, May 31). 31 Powerful Affirmations for every Area of your Life. Medium. https://medium.com/@lizhuberofficial/31-powerful-affirmations-for-every-area-of-your-life-e58aff6a70b2

Hunt, B. (2018, April 25). How To Understand And Overcome Your Limiting Beliefs Around Money. Mind Money Business. https://www.mindmoneybusiness.com.au/limiting-money-beliefs/

John. (2019, October 15). Emotional release visualization to help improve your mental health - La Crisalida Retreats. La Crisalida Retreats. https://lacrisalidaretreats.com/life-makeover/emotional-release-visualisation-improve-mental-health/

LOVE Today. (2022, April 11). Juliette Kristine. Juliette Kristine. https://www.juliettekristine.com/blog/soulmate-affirmations-to-attract-love

Manifest.me1. (2023, October 26). Developing your resilience. Manifest. https://manifest.me/developing-your-resilience/

Manifestation Code 3-6-9. (n.d.). Felicia Bender. https://feliciabender.com/numerology/manifestation-code-3-6-9/

Marks, H. (2023, November 16). Holistic Medicine: What It Is, Treatments, Philosophy, and More. WebMD. https://www.webmd.com/balance/what-is-holistic-medicine

Mastering the 369 Manifestation Method to Achieve Your Dream Life - Centre of Excellence. (2024, February 23). Centreofexcellence.com. https://www.centreofexcellence.com/369-manifestation-method/#1

Mayer, B. A. (2022, February 9). Treat the Whole Self with Holistic Therapy. Healthline. https://www.healthline.com/health/mental-health/holistic-therapy#types

Mayo Clinic Staff. (2020, October 27). How to Build Resiliency. Mayo Clinic. https://www.mayoclinic.org/tests-procedures/resilience-training/in-depth/resilience/art-20046311

Meditative Mind. (2024, June 12). Nicola Tesla's 3-6-9 Theory: What You Need To Know︎. Meditative Mind. https://meditativemind.org/nicola-teslas-3-6-9-theory-what-you-need-to-know/

Migala, J. (2024, January 4). A Step-by-Step Guide to Setting Intentions (and Sticking to Them). The Output. https://www.onepeloton.com/blog/how-to-set-intentions/

Miles, M. (2022, October 25). 8 strategies to collaborate effectively in the workplace. Betterup.com; BetterUp. https://doi.org/106005526/1730395779545/module_84106005526_blog-breadcrumbs

Moe, K. (2021, June 4). 5 visualization techniques to help you reach your goals. Betterup. https://www.betterup.com/blog/visualization

Narbonne, L. (2024, October 14). 100 Powerful Affirmations to Attract Love into Your Life. Innertune Blog | What You Think, You Become. https://blog.innertune.com/attract-love-affirmations/

Nikola Tesla Inventions - Tesla Science Center at Wardenclyffe. (2024, November 18). Tesla Science Center at Wardenclyffe. https://teslasciencecenter.org/nikola-tesla-inventions/#tesla-coil

Pikörn, I. (2020, June 1). What Is Prana & How Can We Feel It? Insight Timer Blog. https://insighttimer.com/blog/what-is-prana/

Porter, A. (n.d.). Looking for motivation to help reach your goals? Try the 369 manifestation method. Www.stylist.co.uk. https://www.stylist.co.uk/fitness-health/wellbeing/how-to-use-369-manifestation-method/552398

Pyne, S. (2023, August 19). The 369 Manifestation Method: The power of number and steps. Hindustan Times.

https://www.hindustantimes.com/astrology/horoscope/the-369-manifestation-method-the-power-of-number-and-steps-101692420055127.html

Raghava K, S. (2023, July 14). Decoding the Enigma of 3, 6, 9: Nikola Tesla Numbers. Medium; Predict. https://medium.com/predict/decoding-the-enigma-3-6-9-nikola-tesla-numbers-45ef6539ef23

Raypole, C. (2021, May 17). Ready, Set, Journal! 64 Journaling Prompts for Self-Discovery. Psych Central. https://psychcentral.com/blog/ready-set-journal-64-journaling-prompts-for-self-discovery#takeaway

Richards, K. (2021, July 28). The Power of Intention in Manifestation. Medium. https://kelli-richards.medium.com/the-power-of-intention-in-manifestation-1172aeb8daf6

Rosenberg, J. (2023, May 8). Intention Setting & Manifestation. Organic India Australia. https://www.organicindia.com.au/blogs/news/intention-setting-manifestation?srsltid=AfmBOooCaDnPHcE_MqG-p7r4c5hnPZQ1bI5XxuY43oeJv6UaIcbUVx-A

Ross, M. (2024, July 9). What Is Manifestation, and Does It Actually Work? We Asked Mental Health Experts. @Onepeloton; Peloton Interactive. https://www.onepeloton.com/blog/what-is-manifesting/

Scott, E. (2020, February 11). How to Practice Loving Kindness Meditation. Verywell Mind. https://www.verywellmind.com/how-to-practice-loving-kindness-meditation-3144786

SEO 2024, A. (2021, April 14). The Benefits of Setting Daily Intentions. Life Purpose Institute. https://lifepurposeinstitute.com/the-benefits-of-setting-daily-intentions/

Short, E. (2022, February 15). What is the 369 Manifestation Method and How to Use it. Mål Paper. https://malpaper.com/blogs/news/what-is-the-369-manifestation-method-and-how-to-use-it?srsltid=AfmBOoomWaCFYZ80O09ccfxet571uvMwhzgu50PHej_LQyJSZEFX7Ypw

Singh, A. N. (2024, February 14). How to manifest love: 10 secrets to attract who you love. Healthshots. https://www.healthshots.com/mind/emotional-health/how-to-manifest-love/

Suga, A. (2024). Insight Timer - #1 Free Meditation App for Sleep, Relax & More. Insighttimer.com. https://insighttimer.com/theilluminary.co/guided-meditations/guided-visualization-to-increase-money-prosperity-wealth

Talbert, S., & Tempera, J. (2022, March 27). The 369 Manifestation Method Has Taken Over TikTok, And TBH, I Can See Why. Women's Health. https://www.womenshealthmag.com/life/a39518396/369-manifestation-method/

Tewari, A. (2023, July 7). 100+ Health Affirmations For A Healthy Body & Mind. Gratitude - the Life Blog. https://blog.gratefulness.me/affirmations-for-health/

The power of setting intentions & how to set mindful ones. (n.d.). Calm Blog. https://www.calm.com/blog/setting-intentions

Torres, E. (2023, January 3). 99 Positive Morning Affirmations You Can Use Daily. The Good Trade. https://www.thegoodtrade.com/features/positive-affirmations-morning-routine/

Tristan. (2021, November 25). Evolve to Grow. Evolve to Grow; Evolve To Grow. https://www.evolvetogrow.com.au/resources/5-money-beliefs-that-are-holding-you-back/#

Velez, H. (2023, January 13). What Is Manifestation? The Good Trade. https://www.thegoodtrade.com/features/what-is-manifestation-how-to/

Visualization meditation: 8 exercises to add to your practice. (2023, August 22). Calm Blog. https://www.calm.com/blog/visualization-meditation

Vyas, N. (2020, May 25). A visualization exercise for mind, body, & Soul Cleansing. Nikita Vyas. https://www.nikitaavyas.in/post/a-visualization-exercise-for-mind-body-soul-cleansing

What is Prana and Why It Matters in Yoga – OmStars. (2024, November 11). Omstars.com. https://omstars.com/blog/practice/what-is-prana-and-why-it-matters-in-yoga/

What is the 369 Method? How the Manifestation Works (2025 Guide) | Reclaim. (2023). Reclaim.ai. https://reclaim.ai/blog/369-method

Williams, D. (2024, September 25). Unlocking the Power of the 369 Method: A Journey into Manifestation with Nikola Tesla's Divine Code. Medium. https://medium.com/@denise_72827/unlocking-the-power-of-the-369-method-a-journey-into-manifestation-with-nikola-teslas-divine-code-50e7b4cad3cc

Zhou, L. (2024, June 26). How to Overcome the 14 Biggest Limiting Beliefs About Money. Luisa Zhou. https://luisazhou.com/blog/limiting-beliefs-about-money/#Money-is-hard-to-make

Part 2: 369 Manifestation Journal

Calm Blog. (2024, July 16). Calm Blog. https://www.calm.com/blog/369-manifestation-method

fcionline. (2019, December 16). 30 affirmations to power happiness and positive thinking. Fertility Centers of Illinois. https://www.fcionline.com/article/30-affirmations-to-power-happiness-and-positive-thinking/

Gupta, S. (n.d.). How to Manifest Your Goals With the 369 Method. Verywell Mind. https://www.verywellmind.com/manifest-your-goals-with-the-369-method-8620625

HowStuffWorks. (2024, October 1). Unlocking the Power of 3, 6, and 9: Exploring the 369 Manifestation Method. HowStuffWorks. https://science.howstuffworks.com/science-vs-myth/extrasensory-perceptions/369-method.htm

Marie, J. (2020, September 14). 23 Affirmations for Joy & Happiness - Janell Marie - Medium. Medium. https://janellmt.medium.com/23-affirmations-for-joy-happiness-d3042204007d

Mastering the 369 Manifestation Method to Achieve Your Dream Life - Centre of Excellence. (2024, February 23). Centreofexcellence.com. https://www.centreofexcellence.com/369-manifestation-method/

Neil, S. (2024, June 13). The 369 Manifestation Method: How-to and Success Tips | Mindset Motive. Mindset Motive. https://mindsetmotive.com/369-manifestation-method/#how-to-succeed-with-the-369-manifestation-method

Pyne, S. (2023, August 19). The 369 Manifestation Method: The power of number and steps. Hindustan Times. https://www.hindustantimes.com/astrology/horoscope/the-369-manifestation-method-the-power-of-number-and-steps-101692420055127.html

Robinson, L., Segal, J., & Smith, M. (2018, October 23). Relaxation Techniques for Stress Relief - HelpGuide.org. HelpGuide.org. https://www.helpguide.org/mental-health/stress/relaxation-techniques-for-stress-relief

Michael, E. (2024, September 26). 120+ Daily Positive Mental Health Affirmations. MentalHealth.com. https://www.mentalhealth.com/tools/positive-mental-health-affirmations

Coach. (2024, February 21). ChantalG. Intuition. ChantalG. Intuition. https://www.chantalg.co.uk/journal-prompts/10-abundance-journal-prompts

Helfand, E. (2021, November 29). The Benefits of Positive Affirmations - Wellspring. Wellspring Center for Prevention. https://wellspringprevention.org/blog/the-benefits-of-positive-affirmations/

How to develop an abundance mindset: 8 tips to help you thrive. (n.d.). Calm Blog. https://www.calm.com/blog/abundance-mindset

Linsey. (2022, April 25). 30 Abundance Journal Prompts to Help You Manifest Your Dreams - Annais. Annais. https://annais.co.uk/abundance-journal-prompts/#google_vignette

Reid, S. (2022, June 6). Gratitude: The Benefits and How to Practice It - HelpGuide.org. HelpGuide.org. https://www.helpguide.org/mental-health/wellbeing/gratitude

Scantalides, A. (2022, January 19). 2 Evening Journal Prompts for a Positive & Abundant Mindset. Aligned & Empowered Coaching; Aligned & Empowered

Coaching. https://ironbodybyartemis.com/2022/01/18/2-evening-journal-prompts-for-a-positive-abundant-mindset/

The power of gratitude: 6 benefits of a gratitude practice. (n.d.). Calm Blog. https://www.calm.com/blog/power-of-gratitude

Well-being, Y., & Youth, Y. (2021, July 2). The Importance of Affirmations. The Y. https://www.ymcansw.org.au/news-and-media/the-y-at-home/the-importance-of-affirmations/

Beachy, L. (2023, May). Law Of Attraction: Aligning Your Thoughts And Actions. Medium. https://medium.com/@lisabeachy/law-of-attraction-aligning-your-thoughts-and-actions-39b7c6223f33

Insight Network, Inc. (2024). Insight Timer - #1 Free Meditation App for Sleep, Relax & More. Insighttimer.com. https://insighttimer.com/murmurr_elixirs/guided-meditations/grounding-and-heart-opening-visualisation

Jenna. (n.d.). 25 Self-Love Journal Prompts. Musings from the Moon. https://musingsfromthemoon.com/blogs/blog/25-self-love-journal-prompts

monerin. (2016, December 23). Self-Love Attracts True Love and Leads to Greater Happiness. How to Be Happy. https://happinessblog.net/self-love-attracts-true-love-and-leads-to-greater-happiness/

Weingus, L. (2021, October 6). 60 Journaling Prompts for Self-Love. Silk + Sonder. https://www.silkandsonder.com/blogs/news/50-journaling-prompts-for-self-love?srsltid=AfmBOop4nHc--OER6_kxf5VcQ0HV8ow44TeRy6FsT6lSBAlBRfq4ZQrP

Houston, M. (2024, December 10). How To Build A Money Mindset For Financial Success In Business And Life. Forbes. https://www.forbes.com/sites/melissahouston/2024/12/10/how-to-build-a-money-mindset-for-financial-success-in-business-and-life/

Joseph, M. (2023, March 10). 52 Reflective Morning Journal Prompts for Inner Peace, Clarity, and Success. Thriving Good Life. https://thrivinggoodlife.com/morning-journal-prompts/

Lyons, Z. (2024, August 30). Mastering Money Mindset: How Your Beliefs Impact Your Financial Decisions. Coachingly.ai. https://www.coachingly.ai/blog/single/mastering-money-mindset-how-your-beliefs-impact-your-financial-decisions

Morrissey, M. (2023, November 9). 111 Journal Prompts for Money Mindset | Money Mindset Shifts 111 Journal Prompts for Money Mindset | Money Mindset Shifts. Brave Thinking Institute. https://www.bravethinkinginstitute.com/blog/life-transformation/journal-prompts-for-money-mindset

Munster, R. (2023, November 10). How Imagining Financial Freedom Can Shape Your Reality. Https://Www.moneyfit.org/. https://www.moneyfit.org/financial-visualization-success/

Hagen, P. (2024, August 21). 47 journal prompts for emotional awareness - Hagen Growth. Hagen Growth. https://hagengrowth.com/journal-prompts-for-emotional-awareness/

James, K. (2024). Insight Timer - #1 Free Meditation App for Sleep, Relax & More. Insighttimer.com. https://insighttimer.com/katejames/guided-meditations/inner-peace-meditation-9

Joseph, M. (2023, March 10). 52 Reflective Morning Journal Prompts for Inner Peace, Clarity, and Success. Thriving Good Life.com. https://thrivinggoodlife.com/morning-journal-prompts/

Pendergast, H. (2023, June). Does positive manifestation for mental well-being work? - Safety and Management Solutions. Safety and Management Solutions. https://www.samsltd.co.uk/does-positive-manifestation-for-mental-well-being-work/

Image Sources

1 Attribution-ShareAlike 3.0 Unported, CC BY-SA 3.0, < https://creativecommons.org/licenses/by-sa/3.0/deed.en> via Wikimedia Commons https://commons.wikimedia.org/wiki/File:Nikola_Tesla_Colored.png

2 https://www.pexels.com/photo/side-view-portrait-photo-of-woman-in-yellow-t-shirt-standing-with-her-eyes-closed-with-trees-in-the-background-2442149/

3 https://www.pexels.com/photo/man-in-black-shorts-sitting-on-floor-4325466/

4 https://www.pexels.com/photo/person-holding-blue-ballpoint-pen-writing-in-notebook-210661/

5 https://www.pexels.com/photo/heart-shaped-red-neon-signage-887349/

6 https://www.pexels.com/photo/happy-woman-in-blue-long-sleeve-blouse-holding-money-7680637/

7 https://www.pexels.com/photo/smiling-woman-looking-upright-standing-against-yellow-wall-1536619/

8 https://www.pexels.com/photo/woman-in-black-top-sitting-on-brown-armchair-3331574/

9 https://www.pexels.com/photo/person-holding-fan-of-us-dollar-bills-4968655/

10 https://www.pexels.com/photo/sitting-blur-reflection-face-6417918/

11 https://www.pexels.com/photo/smiling-woman-in-fur-coat-posing-5922465/

12 https://www.pexels.com/photo/woman-spreading-both-her-arms-2529375/

www.ingramcontent.com/pod-product-compliance
Lightning Source LLC
Chambersburg PA
CBHW051850160426
43209CB00006B/1241